Applied .NET Attributes

TOM BARNABY AND JASON BOCK

Apress™

Applied .NET Attributes
Copyright ©2003 by Tom Barnaby and Jason Bock

ISBN (pbk): 1-59059-136-4

Printed and bound in the United States of America 10987654321

Technical Reviewer: Dan Fergus

Editorial Board: Dan Appleman, Craig Berry, Gary Cornell, Tony Davis, Steven Rycroft, Julian Skinner, Martin Streicher, Jim Sumser, Karen Watterson, Gavin Wray, John Zukowski

Assistant Publisher: Grace Wong

Copy Editor: Marilyn Smith

Production Manager: Kari Brooks

Production Editor: Laura Cheu

Proofreader: Thistle Hill Publishing Services

Compositor: Kinetic Publishing Services, LLC

Indexer: Carol Burbo

Artist: Kinetic Publishing Services, LLC

Cover Designer: Kurt Krames

Manufacturing Manager: Tom Debolski

Distributed to the book trade in the United States by Springer-Verlag New York, Inc., 175 Fifth Avenue, New York, NY, 10010 and outside the United States by Springer-Verlag GmbH & Co. KG, Tiergartenstr. 17, 69112 Heidelberg, Germany.

In the United States: phone 1-800-SPRINGER, email orders@springer-ny.com, or visit http://www.springer-ny.com. Outside the United States: fax +49 6221 345229, email orders@springer.de, or visit http://www.springer.de.

For information on translations, please contact Apress directly at 2560 Ninth Street, Suite 219, Berkeley, CA 94710. Phone 510-549-5930, fax 510-549-5939, email info@apress.com, or visit http://www.apress.com.

The source code for this book is available to readers at http://www.apress.com in the Downloads section. You will need to answer questions pertaining to this book in order to successfully download the code.

Contents at a Glance

Contents

About the Authors

JASON BOCK is a Senior Consultant for Magenic Technologies (http://www.magenic.com). He has worked on a number of business applications using a diverse set of substrates and languages such as C#, .NET, and Java. He is the author of *CIL Programming: Under the Hood of .NET* and *.NET Security*, both published by Apress, and *Visual Basic 6 Win32 API Tutorial*, published by Wrox. He has also written numerous articles on technical development issues. Jason holds both a Bachelor's degree and Master's degree in Electrical Engineering from Marquette University. You can find out more about him at http://www.jasonbock.net.

TOM BARNABY is an instructor and software architect at Intertech Training (http://www.intertech-inc.com), an enterprise developer training firm. Tom is the author of *Distributed .NET Programming in C#* and *Distributed .NET Programming in VB.NET*, published by Apress, and a co-author of *Professional Visual Basic 6 Web Programming*, published by Wrox. Tom is a speaker for the International .NET User Association (INETA) and travels across the country presenting at user group meetings and national developer conferences. Tom graduated with honors from Michigan Technological University with a Bachelor's degree in Computer Science. In his spare time, Tom enjoys playing with his son Max, watching movies, and playing power chords on his electric guitar with the amp volume turned to 11.

Acknowledgments

Jason Bock

First and foremost, I must thank my wife, Liz, for her support and patience as I worked on my material for this book. You're the best. I love you.

I'd like to thank Tom for contributing his clear and concise approach to his sections. I'd also like to thank the wonderful staff at Apress for their support and assistance with this book. People like Gary Cornell, Dan Appleman, Grace Wong, Marilyn Smith, and Laura Cheu (among many others) add a ton of value to their products, and I know that through their help, the content of this book is stronger. Thanks also to Dan Fergus for handling the technical reviews.

Thanks to everyone at Magenic Technologies for letting me work at a place (again!) with talented individuals who really know their stuff. There are a lot of reasons why Magenic is known as one of the top Microsoft-based consulting companies, and I'm glad I work there and can be a part of it. (And the HaloFests are fantastic, although winning the majority of campaigns is getting a bit old . . .)

Finally, to my family and friends, thanks for being there.

Tom Barnaby

As always, I am awed by the amount of work and coordination required to produce a book, even a relatively small one like this. And, once again, I am grateful for the folks at Apress who somehow orchestrate this task. Thanks to Gary Cornell for offering this opportunity and Dan Appleman for his insight and assistance as the project was getting started. Thanks to Marilyn Smith and Dan Fergus for diligently correcting my grammatical and technical lapses, and Laura Cheu for cheerfully leading us through the production cycle. Finally, thanks to Grace Wong for pulling us all together and basically just making things happen.

Thanks to Jason Bock for being the dependable guy he is and driving the process forward in the face of delays.

Thanks to everyone at Intertech Training for providing a challenging and rewarding work environment. Thanks to Tom Salonek and Andrew Troelsen for fostering a culture that encourages both exploration and having fun.

Finally, and most importantly, I'd like to thank my wife, Tammy, and son, Max. The sacrifices I made for this book pale in comparison to yours. Thank you for your patience, love, and support.

Introduction

ATTRIBUTES—WHAT A STRANGE topic to write a book about. We can't tell you how many times we've tried and failed to explain this book. Past books were difficult to describe to relatives and others not in the industry, but this book is unique in that we have trouble explaining it to *other developers*. To many developers, a .NET attribute is just some funny COM IDL-like syntax that you apply to a method to make it a Web method or to expose it to a COM client. "Why?" and "How long is it going to be, 20 pages?" were just a couple of responses we received when disclosing that we were writing a book about .NET attributes.

Joking aside, we believe .NET's attribute concept is one of the most, if not the most, significant feature in .NET. Just look at how Microsoft itself applied attributes within .NET. You will find attributes are key components in COM interoperability, enterprise services, security, serialization, Web services, remoting, and so on. Clearly, Microsoft's developers regard attributes as an extremely useful tool. After reading this book, you will have a solid understanding of how attributes work and why you might want to apply them in your own projects.

What Is Covered

The purpose of this book is to show you how to harness the power of attributes as effectively as Microsoft has. To this end, the book covers not only using the built-in .NET attributes, but also creating custom attributes for your own applications.

Chapters 1 through 3 focus on the basics of attributes and their application within the .NET Framework. These chapters will show you the underlying mechanics of attributes, including how they encapsulate metadata within the CIL code. You will also see how to apply numerous .NET Framework attributes to configure several framework services and to gain an appreciation for the potential of attributes. Because attributes permeate so many aspects of the .NET Framework, these chapters are practically an overview of .NET itself! You will learn about designing custom controls, interoperating with COM and API functions, using code access security, hooking into COM+, serializing objects, and much more.

Chapters 4 and 5 focus on creating and applying custom attributes. These chapters demonstrate how to write your own attributes and how to discover them at runtime using Reflection. You will also learn about a new development philosophy called Aspect Oriented Programming (AOP) and how you can implement AOP using context attributes. The final chapter presents a case study of using custom attributes.

Intended Audience

This book is intended for intermediate to advanced .NET developers. Although the subject matter starts out fairly basic, it quickly accelerates into some complex material. We assume that you are proficient with C# and are familiar with many features of the .NET Framework. We also assume that you are willing and able to consult MSDN (http://msdn.microsoft.com) for the more mundane details.

The Source Code

All of the source code is available for download from the Downloads section of the Apress Web site (http://www.apress.com). The code was compiled and tested using version 1.1 of the .NET Framework, but everything should also work under version 1.0. You can follow most examples using nothing more than the compilers and tools provided in the .NET Framework and a text editor like Notepad. However, we assume Visual Studio .NET is the preferred development tool, and the online code includes Visual Studio .NET project files.

Chapter-by-Chapter Overview

For a more detailed look at the structure and content of this book, let's go over each of the chapters.

Chapter 1: Attribute Fundamentals

This chapter leads you through the underlying implementation of attributes. It explains why metadata is useful and how attributes are converted into metadata and stored within the assembly's CIL code. It also details the syntax of attributes and how to apply attributes to various code items.

Chapter 2: Compile-Time and Design-Time Attributes

This chapter covers several .NET Framework attributes that affect the behavior of the compiler and other .NET tools. You will learn how compile-time attributes can be applied to create conditional method calls, verify CLS or ignore CLS compliance issues, and expose .NET classes to COM components. You will also learn about several design-time attributes, which affect the way Visual Studio .NET displays custom control settings and information.

Chapter 3: Attributes and Runtime Behavior

This chapter surveys several .NET Framework attributes that affect the behavior of the runtime as it executes your code. Ultimately, these attributes allow you to apply .NET code access security, interoperate with COM components and API functions, control the way an object is serialized, and consume COM+ services like automatic transactions.

Chapter 4: Building Custom Attributes

After establishing the usefulness of attributes in the previous chapters, this chapter finally reveals how you can implement your own custom attributes. You will learn how to write custom components that can be applied to code items just like the built-in attributes and how to use .NET Reflection to discover custom attributes at runtime. It also introduces the philosophy of AOP and how you can implement this philosophy using a combination of attributes and .NET's context-interception mechanism.

Chapter 5: Applying Custom Attributes

This chapter is a case study of one possible way to apply custom attributes: implementing checked exceptions (similar to Java's checked exception capability). This will reinforce many of the concepts introduced in Chapter 4 and also demonstrate how to customize the compilation process.

 With the preliminaries complete, let's get started!

CHAPTER 1

Attribute Fundamentals

IN THE COURSE OF DEVELOPING an application, it is quite typical to have core functionality contained in methods that are invoked by other specialized methods. This reduces the spread of code and improves the maintainability of the code base. Similarly, it is routine to move commonly used data to other generalized levels. However, sometimes it becomes apparent that the shared implementations or the data should be published to a level where the implementations or data can be used across other class definitions. This is where metadata comes into play, as object-related services consume this information to provide reusable implementations.

In this chapter, you'll get a tour of the fundamentals of attributes. You'll see how code is dissected to determine when attributes should be used and when other techniques are more applicable. Then you'll be provided with the essentials of attribute-based programming in .NET. You'll understand how attributes are defined and where they can be applied in an assembly. Finally, you'll get a detailed look at where the attribute's information is stored in an assembly.

Applications of Metadata

Attributes are just like any other tool in the developer's proverbial toolkit. They are useful in some situations; in other cases, they can make the solution much more complex than it needs to be. In the following sections, we'll describe how data is used within code and when data is used to define and describe the code base itself.

Defining Data in the Code

Let's start our journey into metadata by looking at some rather simplistic models of a country. The intent is not to have a class that completely describes a country, but to focus on what the code does. Listing 1-1 shows an initial attempt at coding a class that defines a country. As you'll see in a moment, it's not the finest example of writing code.

Listing 1-1. Defining the BadCountry Class

```
namespace Apress.NetAttributes
{
    public class BadCountry
    {
        public string mName;
        public long mPopulation;

        public BadCountry() : base() {}

        public long Population
        {
            get
            {
                return this.mPopulation;
            }
            set
            {
                if(value < 0 ||
                    value > 5000000000000)
                {
                    throw new ArgumentOutOfRangeException(
                        "value", value,
                        "The given value is out of range.");
                }

                this.mPopulation = value;
            }
        }

        public string Name
        {
            get
            {
                return this.mName;
            }
            set
            {
                this.mName = value;
            }
        }
    }
}
```

Seasoned developers can probably find a number of problems with this implementation. However, the key points of contention with this code as it relates to data quality are as follows: *well, it is initial to null*

- The mName field is never initialized. If you create an instance of the BadCountry class and get the Name property, you will have a null reference, which may cause a NullReferenceException.

- Whenever the Population property is set, the given value is checked to ensure it is within a predefined range. However, this range is parameter- ized via hard-coded values (zero and five trillion inclusive). If you wanted to change the range's boundary conditions, you would need to find these values within each occurrence of the range check. Furthermore, there is no way for a BadCountry client to know that the range exists without resort- ing to reverse-engineering techniques.

- The exception message is hard-coded. If you wanted to change the mes- sage, you would need to do this within the property setter itself. Also, there is no way to reuse the message string in another section of code.

- The fields are declared as public, so any data validation that exists (such as the Population setter) can be circumvented with ease.

To address these issues, Listing 1-2 shows a second attempt at constructing a country definition.

Listing 1-2. Improving the BadCountry Definition

```
namespace Apress.NetAttributes
{
    public class ImprovedCountry
    {
        private const string ERROR_ARGUMENT_NAME = "name";
        private const string ERROR_ARGUMENT_POPULATION = "population";
        private const string ERROR_MESSAGE_NULL_VALUE =
            "The given value should not be null.";
        private const string ERROR_MESSAGE_OUT_OF_RANGE =
            "The given value is out of range.";
        public const long MINIMUM_POPULATION = 0;
        public const long MAXIMUM_POPULATION = 5000000000000;

        protected string mName = string.Empty;
        protected long mPopulation;
```

```
    private ImprovedCountry() : base() {}

    public ImprovedCountry(string name, long population)
    {
        this.CheckInvariantName(name);
        this.CheckInvariantPopulation(population);

        this.mName = name;
        this.mPopulation = population;
    }

    protected void CheckInvariantName(string name)
    {
        if(name == null)
        {
            throw new ArgumentNullException(
                ImprovedCountry.ERROR_ARGUMENT_NAME,
                ImprovedCountry.ERROR_MESSAGE_NULL_VALUE);
        }
    }

    protected void CheckInvariantPopulation(long population)
    {
        if(population < ImprovedCountry.MINIMUM_POPULATION ||
            population > ImprovedCountry.MAXIMUM_POPULATION)
        {
            throw new ArgumentOutOfRangeException(
                ImprovedCountry.ERROR_ARGUMENT_POPULATION, population,
                ImprovedCountry.ERROR_MESSAGE_OUT_OF_RANGE);
        }
    }

    public long Population
    {
        get
        {
            return this.mPopulation;
        }
        set
        {
            this.CheckInvariantPopulation(value);
            this.mPopulation = value;
        }
    }
```

```
        public string Name
        {
            get
            {
                return this.mName;
            }
            set
            {
                this.CheckInvariantName(value);
                this.mName = value;
            }
        }
    }
}
```

At first glance, it looks like there is more code involved, and that is true. There are 39 lines in the BadCountry definition and 72 lines in the ImprovedCountry definition. However, the code base has been vastly improved. The fields are now protected, so any changes to their values must be done through the Application Programming Interface (API) set up by ImprovedCountry[1] or via inheritance.

Furthermore, any time the field values need to be changed, validation rules are enforced via calls to either CheckInvariantName() or CheckInvariantPopulation() in the constructor and the setters of both properties. The error messages are now stored in constants and are available for reuse in future version of ImprovedCountry. Finally, the minimum and maximum population values are stored as public constants, so clients will know what the range is before they write even one line of code against an ImprovedCountry instance.

All of these improvements in the code are fairly standard in any refactoring phase. However, these changes don't necessarily make the code bulletproof. We think it's a good idea to move so-called *magic* values (values that just pop up in code) into constants. But the problem with constants is that they are not automatically updated in client code. For example, let's say there was a WinForm application that used the ImprovedCountry class, and it showed the minimum and maximum population values to the user, like this:

```
namespace Apress.NetAttributes
{
    public class CountryClient : System.Windows.Forms.Form
    {
        private System.Windows.Forms.Label lblMaximumPopulationValue;
        private System.Windows.Forms.Label lblMinimumPopulationValue;
```

---

1. It is possible to change the value of a private field via the Reflection API, but we'll ignore that issue for now.

```
public CountryClient()
{
    InitializeComponent();
    this.ShowCountry();
    this.ShowPopulationLimits();
}

private void ShowPopulationLimits()
{
    this.lblMaximumPopulationValue.Text =
        ImprovedCountry.MAXIMUM_POPULATION.ToString();
    this.lblMinimumPopulationValue.Text =
        ImprovedCountry.MINIMUM_POPULATION.ToString();
}

static void Main()
{
    Application.Run(new CountryClient());
}

    //  ...
    }
}
```

Let's say that population increases and improvements in space exploration now require us to change the maximum population.[2]

```
public const long MAXIMUM_POPULATION = 10000000000000;
```

We now take version 2.0.0.0 of the Country assembly and put it into the CountryClient's application directory. Figure 1-1 shows the results of running the application.

---

2. We're assuming that .NET will be around long enough to be used when the colonization of space becomes commonplace.

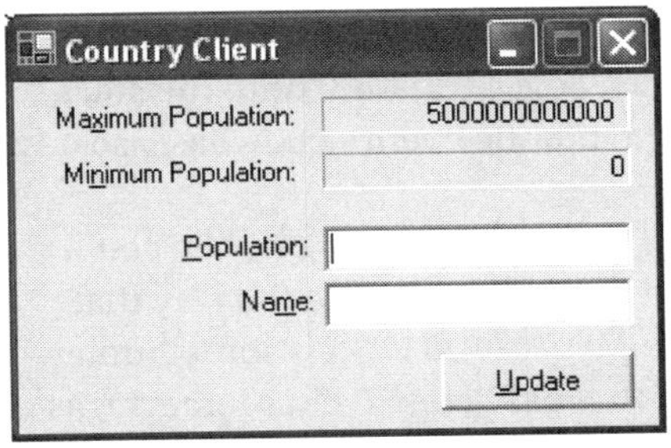

Figure 1-1. Displaying constant values in an updated assembly

The results may surprise you at first glance. Why didn't the client application pick up the new boundary value? The reason is that constant values are embedded into a client assembly at compile-time. Take a look at the resulting Common Intermediate Language (CIL) code[3] that is in ShowPopulationValues().

```
.method private hidebysig instance
  void ShowPopulationLimits() cil managed
{
  .maxstack  2
  .locals init (int64 V_0)
  IL_0000:  ldarg.0
  IL_0001:  ldfld class [System.Windows.Forms]System.Windows.Forms.Label
    Apress.NetAttributes.CountryClient::lblMaximumPopulationValue
  IL_0006:  ldc.i8 0x48c27395000
  IL_000f:  stloc.0
  IL_0010:  ldloca.s V_0
  IL_0012:  call instance string [mscorlib]System.Int64::ToString()
  IL_0017:  callvirt instance void [System.Windows.Forms]
    System.Windows.Forms.Control::set_Text(string)
  IL_001c:  ldarg.0
  IL_001d:  ldfld class [System.Windows.Forms]System.Windows.Forms.Label
    Apress.NetAttributes.CountryClient::lblMinimumPopulationValue
  IL_0022:  ldc.i4.0
  IL_0023:  conv.i8
  IL_0024:  stloc.0
  IL_0025:  ldloca.s V_0
  IL_0027:  call instance string [mscorlib]System.Int64::ToString()
  IL_002c:  callvirt instance void [System.Windows.Forms]
    System.Windows.Forms.Control::set_Text(string)
  IL_0031:  ret
}
```

---

3. If you're not familiar with CIL, one of the authors of this book, Jason Bock, has written a book on this base language of .NET: *CIL Programming: Under the Hood of .NET* (Apress, 2002).

The lines that are of particular importance are IL_0006 and IL_0022. The value, 0x48c27395000, is 5,000,000,000,000, and ldc.i4.0 loads 0 onto the stack. Essentially, the constant values are hard-coded into the client's code base, so any updates go unnoticed.[4]

Again, constants are not necessarily a bad thing. But creating public constants does not mean that clients will ever use those constants in the way that the implementer intended. Naming a field MAXIMUM_POPULATION has some human-based semantics,[5] but it's up to a client to use that field effectively. Moreover, as you have just seen, constants do not have a good versioning story. Sometimes, it's advantageous to have data that can be versioned and is accessible to a client. As you'll see in the "Attributes in .NET" section later in this chapter, attributes have these properties.

Defining Data About the Code

As with anything that is associated with data, there comes a time when an object's information will need to be persisted so it can be retrieved (and possibly updated) in the future. One approach is to have a client determine how the object's state should be saved. Listing 1-3 demonstrates one possible implementation.

Listing 1-3. Saving a Country Object

```
private void btnSave_Click(object sender, System.EventArgs e)
{
    if(this.mCountry != null)
    {
        TextWriter countryFile =
            File.CreateText(Application.StartupPath +
            @"\country.txt");

        try
        {
            countryFile.WriteLine(
                "name:{0}", this.mCountry.Name);
            countryFile.WriteLine(
                "population:{0}", this.mCountry.Population);
        }
        finally
```

---

4. This is done for performance reasons. It's a lot faster to simply load a value than it is to read it from a field in either a class or an object.

5. This is especially true for those who can read English.

```
        {
            countryFile.Close();
        }
    }
}
```

Figure 1-2 shows what a typical country.txt file would look like in Notepad.

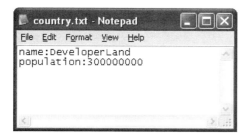

Figure 1-2. Persisting an ImprovedCountry object

However, this implementation is just one way to save the data to a file. What if another client application decides to save it to an XML file? What if the second client chooses to store the Population's property value first? Persistence strategies can vary widely among applications. The only chance of interoperability between these formats is solid documentation.

One way to improve this approach is to create an interface that a class can implement so it can control the serialization process:

```
public interface IPersist
{
    void Load(Stream persistenceTarget);
    void Save(Stream persistenceTarget);
}
```

To illustrate how this interface could be implemented, we'll create a new class named PersistedCountry that has ImprovedCountry as its base class. It will also implement the IPersist interface. Listing 1-4 shows the implementation of PersistedCountry.

Listing 1-4. Implementing PersistedCountry

```
public class PersistedCountry : ImprovedCountry, IPersist
{
    private const string NAME_KEY = "name";
    private const string POPULATION_KEY = "population";
```

```
        public PersistedCountry(string name, long population) :
            base(name, population) {}

        public void Load(Stream persistenceTarget)
        {
            int totalBytes = (int)persistenceTarget.Length;
            Decoder dec = (new UnicodeEncoding()).GetDecoder();
            byte[] storedInfo = new byte[totalBytes];
            persistenceTarget.Read(storedInfo, 0, totalBytes);
            char[] storedChars = new char[dec.GetCharCount(
                storedInfo, 0, totalBytes)];
            int totalDecodedChars = dec.GetChars(storedInfo, 0, totalBytes,
                storedChars, 0);
            string info = new string(storedChars);

            int nameStart = info.IndexOf(NAME_KEY);
            int populationStart = info.IndexOf(POPULATION_KEY);

            this.mName = info.Substring(nameStart + NAME_KEY.Length + 1,
                populationStart - (nameStart + NAME_KEY.Length));
            this.mPopulation = Int32.Parse(
                info.Substring(populationStart + POPULATION_KEY.Length + 1));
        }

        public void Save(Stream persistenceTarget)
        {
            Encoding enc = new UnicodeEncoding();
            string nameInfo = string.Format("{0}:{1}", NAME_KEY, this.mName);
            byte[] nameInfoBytes = enc.GetBytes(nameInfo);
            persistenceTarget.Write(nameInfoBytes, 0,
                nameInfoBytes.Length);
            string populationInfo = string.Format("{0}:{1}",
                POPULATION_KEY, this.Population);
            byte[] populationInfoBytes = enc.GetBytes(populationInfo);
            persistenceTarget.Write(populationInfoBytes, 0,
                populationInfoBytes.Length);
        }
    }
```

This will centralize how the ImprovedCountry object will save its information, but there is still the problem of consistency. One class may decide to use XML; another might use a binary format. Furthermore, there is no chance to share these persistence mechanisms among class definitions as long as they remain internal to the object.

If we alter IPersist's methods to take an object that stores name/value pairs instead of a Stream-based object, the object is responsible only for storing the data that it wants to retain. To illustrate this, we'll overload Load() and Save() to take a Hashtable reference.

```
public interface IPersist
{
    void Load(Stream persistenceTarget);
    void Load(Hashtable nameValuePairs);
    void Save(Stream persistenceTarget);
    void Save(Hashtable nameValuePairs);
}
```

This reduces the burden of the implementer of IPersist significantly.

```
public void Load(Hashtable nameValuePairs)
{
    if(nameValuePairs != null)
    {
        if(nameValuePairs.Contains(NAME_KEY))
        {
            this.mName = (string)nameValuePairs[NAME_KEY];
        }
        if(nameValuePairs.Contains(POPULATION_KEY))
        {
            this.mPopulation = (long)nameValuePairs[POPULATION_KEY];
        }
    }
}

public void Save(Hashtable nameValuePairs)
{
    if(nameValuePairs != null)
    {
        nameValuePairs.Add(NAME_KEY, this.mName);
        nameValuePairs.Add(POPULATION_KEY, this.mPopulation);
    }
}
```

The client would now persist an ImprovedCountry object by using another object to house the storage-strategy code.

```
public interface IObjectStorage
{
    void Load(IPersist targetObject, FileStream stream);
    void Save(IPersist targetObject, FileStream stream);
}
```

Now the serialization apparatus is generalized, not specific to how one object decides to do it.

 NOTE *At this point, the design is starting to take on the trappings of the serialization classes in .NET. It's nowhere near as comprehensive, but the point of this discussion is not to repeat the designs of the .NET Framework, so we'll stop here.*

We can take this one step further. Most of the time, an object will store its field values during a serialization process. Via Reflection, code can be written to read an object's fields (public, private, or otherwise) in a general fashion that is independent of the object's type.[6]

```
public void PokeAtObject(object targetObject)
{
    FieldInfo[] fields = targetObject.GetType().GetFields(
        BindingFlags.Public | BindingFlags.NonPublic |
        BindingFlags.Instance);

    foreach(FieldInfo field in fields)
    {
        string fieldName = field.Name;
        object fieldValue = field.GetValue(targetObject);
    }
}
```

In this case, there is no reason for an object to implement IPersist, because it does not need to customize the serialization process. Granted, object persistence is not as easy as this. For example, the Reflection code doesn't take into consideration deep object graphs; it just looks at the fields contained within a given object. Furthermore, some objects may have specialized needs that simple field iteration won't handle, so having the IPersist interface is a good thing. It should, however, not be a requirement for a class that wants its instances to be

---

6. Such access requires high privileges, which is accounted for in .NET's security architecture.

persistable to implement an interface. This is where using attributes can be beneficial. Attributes are useful to define public data about an assembly's members that can be used by object-related services to perform generalized tasks.

Another example of where attributes are useful is when you need to mark either methods or entire classes as obsolete. If it were just one method, a developer could have the method throw a NotSupportedException, but clients of that object would get an unexpected surprise when they called that method. Also, there is no way to warn the client of future obsolescence. An attribute could be used on a method or an entire class to state that other paths should be used in the near future. Plus, an attribute can be constructed to provide fair warning without causing unexpected behavior.

Defining Data Outside the Code

There is one last place where we can put data that defines our code: in a configuration file. This is nothing new. Long-time Windows developers have used INI files to store application-related information like user preferences, FTP site locations, and so on. Now it's conceivable that you could store metadata in configuration files. For example, here's what a configuration file would look like if we needed to state that BadCountry was obsolete:

```
<BadCountry>
    <Metadata>
        <Obsolete CausesError="True"/>
    </Metadata>
</BadCountry>
```

The runtime would need to look up the information in the configuration file whenever a serialization request was made to make sure that the designer of the class allows its instances to be persisted.

However, there are problems with this approach. First, with the metadata outside the code base, you now have an installation issue. Having the metadata in an XML file means that you must ship two files to the client. When the metadata is in the assembly, you need to ship only one file. This may not sound like a big deal, but at least with the one-file approach (assembly-only), you know the metadata is there when the assembly is there.

Another problem is with metadata inheritance. As you'll see in the "Attribute Targets" section later in this chapter, as well as the "Inheritance and Custom Attributes" section in Chapter 4, you can set up attributes so that their use on a base class will also affect subclasses. You could do this with configuration files as well, but this kind of behavior is not designed into .NET. Code that acts on metadata would need to consider the lookup of the information within a base class; this is automatically taken care of through the design of attributes in .NET.

The bigger issue is that external metadata can be adjusted by a client with relative ease. Would you want someone to make a class that was obsolete relevant again? What about making a class serializable when it was never intended to be saved to disk? When the metadata is in the assembly, it's much harder for someone to change that metadata. The intentions of the designer have a better chance of being preserved when they're embedded within the compiler's output.

> **NOTE**   *Granted, we're not dealing with reverse-engineering scenarios here. Someone who is savvy enough with ILDasm and CIL could make an obsolete class nonobsolete rather easily. There are countermeasures to reverse-engineering, but that discussion goes well beyond the topic at hand.*

Don't get us wrong—configuration files can be useful, especially when they define values that are used by the code and may change after the code is compiled. But configuration files are not appropriate when they define design characteristics of the class itself. Attributes are tightly coupled to the element that they are associated with, which is an essential feature of metadata.

You've now seen where attributes can be used effectively. Now it's time to see how attributes are used in C#.

Attributes in .NET

Using attributes in your .NET code is fairly straightforward, but knowing the rules will not only help you to understand why some compilation errors may occur when you code with attributes, but it will also guide you when you create your own attributes (a topic we'll cover in Chapter 4). In this section, you'll learn how you declare attributes in your C# code, where and when attributes can be declared, and where the attribute information ends up.

Declaration Fundamentals

To demonstrate how attributes are used in C# code, we'll use the ObsoleteAttribute class to mark our BadCountry class as a class that clients should no longer use, but it will not cause an error to use BadCountry. Listing 1-5 shows the code necessary to do this.

Listing 1-5. Making a Class Obsolete via Attributes

```
[Obsolete]
public class BadCountry
{
    // ...
}
```

Attributes are declared within the brackets. Only objects whose class inherits from System.Attribute can be used within the brackets. For example, the following code would cause an error:

```
[DateTime(2003, 2, 19)]
public class BadCountry
{
    // ...
}
```

Attributes are usually named with the string "Attribute" at the end. You are not required to type in the full name when you add the attribute to your code,[7] but you can if you prefer, as shown here:

```
[ObsoleteAttribute]
public class BadCountry
{
    // ...
}
```

When you add an attribute in your code, you are technically creating a new object whose information will be stored in the assembly. If the attribute has a no-argument constructor, you don't need to use parentheses in your declaration. However, as is the case with ObsoleteAttribute, attributes can define custom constructors so you can set the state of the attribute with more detail. The following code snippet uses a custom constructor of ObsoleteAttribute to set a string and boolean value.

---

7. This is primarily done to reduce name collisions between attribute and normal class definitions within an assembly.

```
[Obsolete("This class should no longer be used - switch to ImprovedCountry.",
    false)]
public class BadCountry
{
    //  ...
}
```

In this case, the string argument (called message) is used to define a descriptive message that clients can use to find other alternative implementations. The boolean argument (called error) is used during the client's compilation process. A true value will cause a compilation error if the deprecated item is still used; a false value will cause a compilation warning. Figure 1-3 shows the compilation output in Visual Studio .NET when BadCountry is used with error set to false.

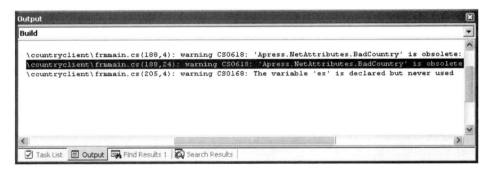

Figure 1-3. Compilation warning messages when using ObsoleteAttribute

However, as Figure 1-4 demonstrates, when error is set to true, the client code won't even compile.

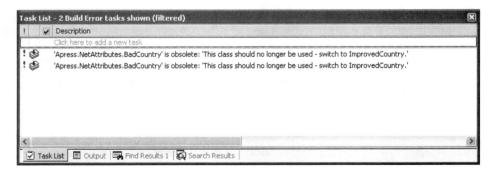

Figure 1-4. Compilation error messages when using ObsoleteAttribute

Not all attributes will affect the compilation process as `ObsoleteAttribute` does. In fact, attributes in themselves are harmless, *unless* some other process, like a compiler or the Common Language Runtime (CLR), acts on them. Although attributes will end up in your assembly, they cannot affect your code.[8]

NOTE *Other factors are involved in using an attribute's information and acting accordingly. Chapters 2 and 3 will cover different attributes and when they come into play.*

Attribute Targets

So far, you've seen how an attribute is declared in C# code to affect a class definition. However, attributes can be applied to nearly any part of a .NET assembly. When you declare an attribute as shown in Listing 1-5, the attribute is applied to the class, rather than to any of the class's methods or fields. If you want to make the target of an attribute explicit, you can prefix the attribute declaration with the target name by adding the `type` keyword, as Listing 1-6 shows.

Listing 1-6. Explicitly Stating the Attribute Target

```
[type: Obsolete(
    "This class should no longer be used - switch to ImprovedCountry.",
    true)]
public class BadCountry
{
    // ...
}
```

When an attribute is defined, it can also state the valid targets that it can be applied to in code. This is done via the `AttributeTargets` enumeration. Table 1-1 describes all of the values in the `AttributeTargets` enumeration.

---

8. Of course, this is not true if a compiler is designed to read attributes to emit code during the compilation process.

Table 1-1. Valid Attribute Targets

AttributeTargets Name	Description
All	All application elements
Assembly	Assembly level
Class	All classes
Constructor	All constructors
Delegate	All delegates
Enum	All enumerations
Event	All events
Field	All fields
Interface	All interfaces
Method	All methods
Module	All modules
Parameter	All method arguments
Property	All properties
ReturnValue	All method return values
Struct	All value types

The values of AttributeTargets can be ORed together, so an attribute designer can make any combination of valid targets. The All value is supplied if an attribute can be applied to any target. C# defines nine keywords that can be used to apply the attribute to a specific target in code: assembly, event, field, method, module, param, property, return, and type. As you can guess, some of these keywords overlap with the values in AttributeTargets. For example, type can be used on a class, an interface, a structure, an enumeration, and a delegate definition; param can be used on only method arguments.

Where an attribute can be legally applied is determined by the implementer of the attribute. An attribute designer uses the AttributeTargetsAttribute class on the attribute definition itself to control the attribute's valid destinations. (We'll cover AttributeTargetsAttribute in detail in Chapter 4.) For example, if you need to make only one method of BadCountry obsolete, you apply the attribute like this:

```
[property: Obsolete("This is a bad property.",
    true)]
public long Population
{
    // ...
}
```

However, you cannot make an entire assembly obsolete. The following C#
code will cause a compilation error:[9]

```
[assembly: Obsolete(
    "This assembly should no longer be used.",
    true)]
```

Furthermore, the location of the attribute when a target is explicitly given is also
important. For example, an assembly-level attribute (like AssemblyTitleAttribute)
cannot be declared inside a class or namespace; it must exist outside these scopes,
as the following code snippet demonstrates:

```
//  This is OK.
[assembly: AssemblyTitle("Country assembly.")]

namespace Apress.NetAttributes
{
    //  This isn't.
    [assembly: AssemblyTitle("Country assembly.")]

    public class BadCountry
    {
        //  Neither is this.
        [assembly: AssemblyTitle("Country assembly.")]
    }
}
```

You're not limited to applying only one attribute to a given target. For example, the following code is valid:

---

9. The .NET Framework SDK will list in an attribute's definition which targets are valid.

```
[type: Obsolete(
    "This class should no longer be used - switch to ImprovedCountry.",
    true)]
[type: Serializable]
public class BadCountry
{
    // ...
}
```

You may, however, be limited in terms of how many times you can apply one *specific* attribute to a particular target. For example, the following code will not compile:

```
[type: Obsolete("This class should no longer be used - switch to ImprovedCountry.",
    true)]
[type: Obsolete("Really - don't use this class!",
    true)]
public class BadCountry
{
    // ...
}
```

As with the valid target locations, an attribute designer can control if an attribute can be applied to same target multiple times via the AllowMultiple property of the AttributeUsageAttributes class. The default behavior for an attribute is that it will not be a multiuse attribute, because it is unusual for an attribute to be applied to the same target multiple times, but this can be changed.

Finally, attributes can control whether or not their information is inherited in subclasses or overridden methods. For example, let's say we tried to use BadCountry as a base class.

```
[type: Obsolete("Really - don't use this class!",
    true)]
public class BadCountry
{
    // ...
}


//  This will not compile.
public class BadInheritedCountry : BadCountry
{
    // ...
}
```

In this case, the code won't compile because BadInheritedCountry is trying to use an obsolete class. However, if we didn't set error to true in ObsoleteAttribute's constructor, not only would the code compile, but clients would be able to do this without getting a warning.

```
BadInheritedCountry bic = new BadInheritedCountry();
```

ObsoleteAttribute was designed so that its information does not flow to a subclass. However, this choice is up to the creator of the attribute. Again, AttributeUsageAttributes is the center of control to determine how an attribute's information flows in inheritance scenarios. The default behavior is for attributes to be inheritable,[10] but an attribute can be limited to the target to which it is applied. We'll come back to these design issues in the "Inheritance and Custom Attributes" section in Chapter 4.

You now know how attributes work in C#. But the story doesn't stop there. When you compile your attribute-laden code, the metadata ends up in the assembly in one form or another. In the next section, you'll see where the attribute is located in an assembly and how that information is stored.

Compiling Attributes

Fortunately, from a compilation perspective, there is nothing that you need to do differently when you include attributes in your C# code. You don't need to check a check box in Visual Studio .NET or add a switch to csc.exe to have your attributes show up in the resulting assembly. For example, if you look at an assembly that contains attributes in ILDasm, you'll see something that looks like Figure 1-5.

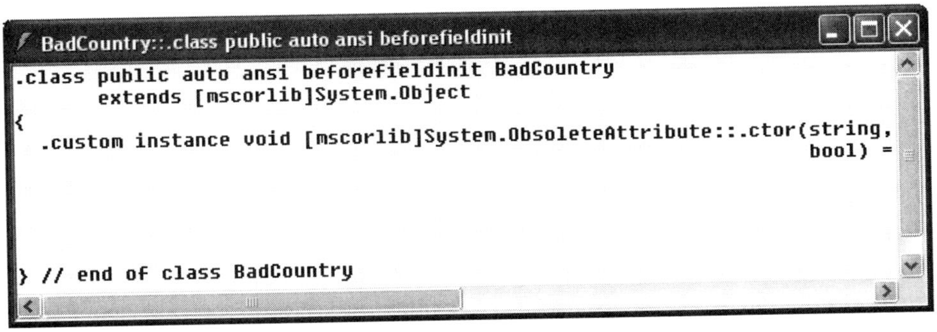

```
BadCountry::.class public auto ansi beforefieldinit
.class public auto ansi beforefieldinit BadCountry
       extends [mscorlib]System.Object
{
  .custom instance void [mscorlib]System.ObsoleteAttribute::.ctor(string,
                                                                  bool) =

} // end of class BadCountry
```

Figure 1-5. The .custom directives in an assembly

---

10. This has nothing to do with whether or not the attribute *class* is sealed.

The custom attribute will be stored within a `.custom` directive. The location of the directive will vary depending on the target stated in the C# code. In this case, `ObsoleteAttribute` was used on the `BadCountry` class. The directive will state the full name of the attribute type, along with the constructor used in the attribute declaration. Unfortunately, space limitations prevented us from showing the full story in Figure 1.5. There is something after the equal sign that couldn't fit in the image. Listing 1-7 shows what ends up on the other side.

Listing 1-7. The Full Attribute Format in an Assembly

```
.class public auto ansi beforefieldinit BadCountry
   extends [mscorlib]System.Object
{
  .custom instance void
    [mscorlib]System.ObsoleteAttribute::.ctor(string,
    bool) =
      ( 01 00 40 54 68 69 73 20 63 6C 61 73 73 20 73 68   // ..@This class sh
       6F 75 6C 64 20 6E 6F 20 6C 6F 6E 67 65 72 20 62   // ould no longer b
       65 20 75 73 65 64 20 2D 20 73 77 69 74 63 68 20   // e used - switch
       74 6F 20 49 6D 70 72 6F 76 65 64 43 6F 75 6E 74   // to ImprovedCount
       72 79 2E 01 00 00 )                               // ry....
} // end of class BadCountry
```

You can glean some general ideas as to what the bytes represent, but you do not need to know the full details of the format to use and create attributes successfully. As you'll see in Chapter 4, the API to read metadata from an assembly is rather straightforward and does not require you to know the layout of the byte array.

> **NOTE** *For those who are curious to know what the bytes stand for, Appendix of this book goes through the format in excruciating detail.*

Most attributes will end up in a `.custom` directive. Interestingly enough, they are known as *custom* attributes. However, there is a special set of attributes that, when present in code, will end up in other places in the assembly. These are known as *pseudo-custom* attributes.[11] You declare them in the same way that you

---

11. See Section 20.2.1 of Partition II for more details on pseudo-custom attributes. Note that some pseudo-custom attributes are not CLS-compliant, so take care if you use them in your code.

declare any other attribute in your C# code, but the end results in the assembly are vastly different. For example, take a look at the following code:

```
[assembly: AssemblyVersion("1.0.0.0")]
```

When you compile your code, you won't find a .custom directive with a type name that contains AssemblyVersionAttribute. Figure 1-6 shows what happens when you use AssemblyVersionAttribute.

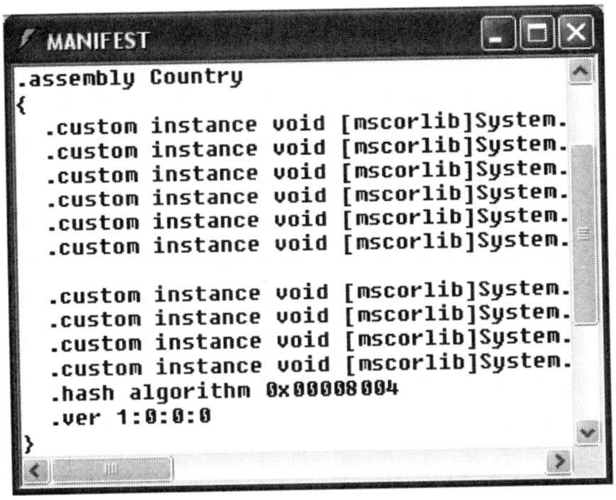

Figure 1-6. Pseudo-custom attributes in assemblies

In this case, the .ver directive contains the version information of the assembly.

There is a reason why pseudo-custom attributes are stored in this fashion: it's more efficient. Pseudo-custom attributes don't have the overhead of storing a bunch of bytes that a normal custom attribute requires. An explicit example of this is when you make a class serializable, like this:

```
[type: Serializable]
public class SerializableCountry
{
    // ...
}
```

The ILDasm results are as follows:

```
.class public auto ansi serializable beforefieldinit SerializableCountry
  extends [mscorlib]System.Object
{
} // end of class SerializableCountry
```

Notice that the `serializable` attribute now ends up in the class definition. There is no `.custom` directive anywhere on the class. What is really going on is that a bit flag is being set for `SerializableCountry`. When you use the `SerializableAttribute` attribute with the class, here's what the token looks like:[12]

```
TypDefName: Apress.NetAttributes.SerializableCountry   (02000008)
Flags      : [Public] [AutoLayout] [Class] [Serializable] [AnsiClass]   (00102001)
```

Without the `SerializableAttribute` attribute, you'll notice that a value in the Flags field changes:

```
TypDefName: Apress.NetAttributes.SerializableCountry   (02000008)
Flags      : [Public] [AutoLayout] [Class] [AnsiClass]   (00100001)
```

Pseudo-custom attributes have this special storage consideration because they are used extensively by compilers or by the CLR. It's much faster for the CLR to look at a bit field to see if it's serializable, rather than to go through all of the custom attributes (if any exist) to see if one of them is of the `SerializableAttribute` type. Of course, with this efficiency comes a trade-off in verbosity. A class is either serializable or it's not serializable. Contrast that with the `ObsoleteAttribute`, which lets you give a client a helpful message and make obsolete elements cause either a warning or an error during compilation.

SOURCE CODE   *The code for these examples is in Chapter1\Country and Chapter1\CountryClient.*

---

12. You can see these flag values (along with a lot more juicy metadata information) if you start up ILDasm with the /adv switch. A Metadata option will appear on the View menu, which you can use to view the token and flag values.

Conclusion

In this chapter, you learned the following about attributes:

- Where data can be stored in and around code, and how that compares to attributes

- How to declare attributes within C# code

- Where attributes end up in an assembly

In the next chapter, you'll get the details on how some attributes are used directly during the compilation process and the effects of using these attributes.

CHAPTER 2

Compile-time and Design-time Attributes

As noted in Chapter 1, attributes must be recognized and acted upon by a consuming application. In many cases, this consuming application will be the .NET runtime. Chapter 3 covers many of the attributes that affect runtime behavior. In this chapter, we will focus on those attributes that affect the behavior of the compiler and other tools such as tlbimp, regasm, regsvcs, and even Visual Studio .NET.

Compiler Attributes

Technically speaking, all attributes affect compiler behavior in that the compiler responds by inserting the appropriate metadata in the assembly. Beyond this, however, certain attributes are specifically designed to affect the compiler behavior in other ways. This section reviews a couple of these compiler-targeted attributes.

The CLSCompliant Attribute

One of the hallmarks of the .NET Framework is the ability to build assemblies in multiple languages and have all the assemblies interoperate seamlessly. To facilitate this capability, the .NET Framework is built on two fundamental specifications: the Common Type System (CTS) and the Common Language Specification (CLS). The CTS specifies a large number of features and primitive data types that a .NET language can choose to support. The CLS is a subset of the CTS, meaning that a language feature may be fine by CTS standards but be outside the realm of the CLS. Whenever you choose to use such a feature, you must be aware of the possible interoperability issues it may cause, because .NET does not guarantee that other .NET assemblies will be able to consume a non-CLS-compliant item.

For example, C# allows you to define and use unsigned numerical types such as an unsigned integer (uint). Although this falls within the CTS guidelines, it is outside the scope of the CLS. Keep in mind that the CLS rules apply only to items that an assembly exposes to other .NET assemblies. Therefore, using an unsigned type in C# does not pose any interoperability issues, provided that you do not expose it outside the assembly. If you do expose it outside the assembly, however, some .NET languages may not be able to effectively consume your assembly. In order to help .NET developers avoid this situation, the .NET Framework provides the CLSCompliant attribute. With this attribute, you can control the compiler's response to publicly exposed non-CLS-compliant items by telling the compiler to issue an error or to ignore the offending item.

For example, the code in Listing 2-1 contains some potential CLS-compliant issues.

Listing 2-1. Testing CLS Compliance

```
public class ComplianceTest
{
    // The uint type is non-CLS compliant. But since
    // this field is private, the CLS rules do not apply.
    private uint a = 4;

    // Since this uint field is public, we have a CLS
    // compliance issue.
    public uint B = 5;

    // This is the correct way to expose an uint; The
    // long type is CLS compliant.
    public long A
    {
        get { return a; }
    }
}
```

Normally, this code compiles without any errors, despite the publicly exposed unsigned integer. However, since it can cause interoperability issues with other .NET assemblies, you may wish the compiler to catch this and generate an error. In this case, you can apply the CLSCompliant attribute. Although you can apply this attribute to any type of code item, it is typically applied to the assembly to indicate that the compiler should verify that everything in the assembly is CLS-compliant, as follows:

```
[assembly: CLSCompliant(true)]
```

 NOTE *The standard location for applying attributes to the assembly is the AssemblyInfo.cs file. This file is automatically generated when you create a new project with Visual Studio .NET.*

Now when you compile Listing 2-1, the compiler issues the error shown in Figure 2-1.

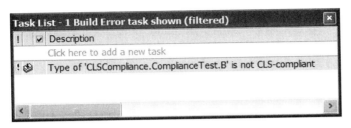

Figure 2-1. *The CLS-compliant compiler error*

At times, you may wish the compiler to ignore a noncompliant item, even if you have applied the CLSCompliant attribute to the entire assembly. In this case, you can apply the CLSCompliant attribute to the containing type or directly to the item itself, while passing false into the attribute constructor. This is demonstrated in Listing 2-2.

Listing 2-2. *Turning Off CLS-Compliance Checking on a Type*

```
[CLSCompliant(false)] // Ignore CLS compliant issues in this class
public class ComplianceTest
{
    // The uint type is non-CLS compliant. But since
    // this field is private, the CLS rules do not apply.
    private uint a = 4;

    // Since this uint field is public, we have a CLS
    // compliance issue.
    public uint B = 5;

    // This is the correct way to expose an uint; The
    // long type is CLS compliant.
    public long A
    {
        get { return a; }
    }
}
```

When this code is compiled, the compiler will ignore the public unsigned integer field.

The Conditional Attribute

Developers often surround tracing and debugging code with conditional compilation directives such as #define, #if, #else, and #endif. This allows the code to be
easily removed when the final release version is compiled. Most .NET languages
support these conditional compilation directives, but the .NET Framework also
supplies the Conditional attribute in the System.Diagnostics namespace.

The Conditional attribute allows you to mark a method as a *conditional
method*, which can be called conditionally based on the definition of a symbol.
Unlike compilation directives, however, the Conditional attribute verifies that
a given symbol is defined by the *calling* code. If the symbol is undefined when
the calling code invokes the conditional method, the compiler removes the
method call. For example, consider the code in Listing 2-3, which defines a custom tracing class.

Listing 2-3. Applying the Conditional Attribute

```
namespace TraceLibrary
{
    public class CustomTrace
    {
        [Conditional("CUSTOM_TRACING")]
        public static void Write(TextWriter tw, string msg)
        {
            tw.WriteLine("{0}: {1}", DateTime.Now, msg);
        }
    }
}
```

The Write() method in this example implements a simple tracing mechanism
that writes a message to the given TextWriter object (the Console.Out property, for
example, returns a TextWriter object) with a prepended timestamp. To allow developers to easily remove calls to the CustomTrace.Write() method, it is marked with the
Conditional attribute. The string passed into the attribute constructor specifies
the name of the symbol that the calling code must define to call the method.

To see the effect this attribute has on the compiler, consider the code in
Listing 2-4.

Listing 2-4. Testing the Conditional Attribute

```
using System;
using TraceLibrary;

namespace ConditionalTest
{
    class MainApp
    {
        static void Main(string[] args)
        {
            CustomTrace.Write(Console.Out, "Starting Main");
            Console.WriteLine("Doing work in Main");
            CustomTrace.Write(Console.Out, "Leaving Main");
        }
    }
}
```

This example calls the `CustomTrace.Write()` method a couple times. However, notice that this code does not define the `CUSTOM_TRACING` symbol. Therefore, the output shows only the "Doing work in main" message, as shown in Figure 2-2.

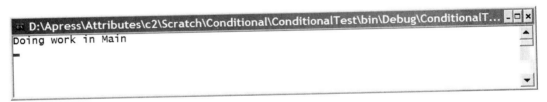

Figure 2-2. Listing 2-4 output without defining CUSTOM_TRACING

This behavior is not some trick of the runtime. Instead, the C# compiler completely removed the conditional method calls from the code in `Main()`. You can see this in Listing 2-5, which shows the CIL code resulting from compiling the code in Listing 2-4. Notice that the calls to `CustomTrace.Write()` are missing!

Listing 2-5. The CIL Code Generated from Listing 2-4 (Without Defining CUSTOM_TRACING)

```
.method private hidebysig static void  Main(string[] args) cil managed
{
  .entrypoint
  // Code size       11 (0xb)
```

31

```
      .maxstack  1
      IL_0000:  ldstr      "Doing work in main"
      IL_0005:  call       void [mscorlib]System.Console::WriteLine(string)
      IL_000a:  ret
} // end of method MainApp::Main
```

To enable the CustomTrace.Write() method calls, you need to define the CUSTOM_TRACING symbol at some point prior to calling the methods. You can do this with a #define compiler directive, as shown here:

```
#define CUSTOM_TRACING   // Turn on custom tracing calls in this file
```

Alternatively, you can define the symbol using the /define compiler switch or by setting it in Visual Studio .NET's project properties window, as shown in Figure 2-3.

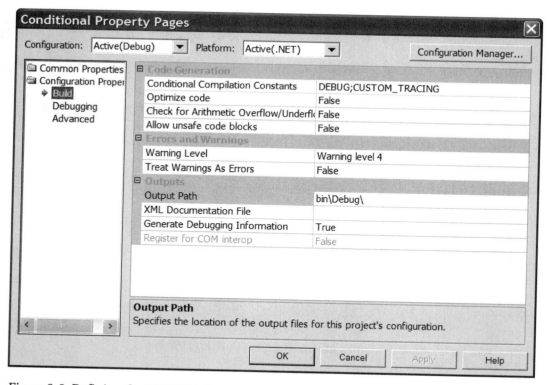

Figure 2-3. Defining the CUSTOM_TRACING symbol within Visual Studio .NET

With the `CUSTOM_TRACING` symbol now defined, the compiler includes the calls to `CustomTracing.Write()`. You can see this in the resulting CIL, shown in Listing 2-6.

Listing 2-6. The CIL Generated from Listing 2-4 with CUSTOM_TRACING Defined

```
.method private hidebysig static void  Main(string[] args) cil managed
{
  .entrypoint
  // Code size       41 (0x29)
  .maxstack  2
  IL_0000:  call        class [mscorlib]System.IO.TextWriter
                            [mscorlib]System.Console::get_Out()
  IL_0005:  ldstr       "Starting Main"
  IL_000a:  call        void [TraceLibrary]TraceLibrary.CustomTrace::Write(
                            class [mscorlib]System.IO.TextWriter, string)
  IL_000f:  ldstr       "Doing work in main"
  IL_0014:  call        void [mscorlib]System.Console::WriteLine(string)
  IL_0019:  call        class [mscorlib]System.IO.TextWriter
                            [mscorlib]System.Console::get_Out()
  IL_001e:  ldstr       "Leaving Main"
  IL_0023:  call        void [TraceLibrary]TraceLibrary.CustomTrace::Write(
                            class [mscorlib]System.IO.TextWriter, string)
  IL_0028:  ret
} // end of method MainApp::Main
```

You can also see the difference in the program output, shown in Figure 2-4.

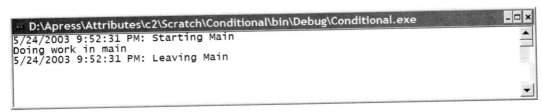

Figure 2-4. Listing 2-4 output with CUSTOM_TRACING defined

SOURCE CODE   *The code for this example is in Chapter2\Conditional.*

Assembly Attributes

The .NET Framework provides many attributes that allow you to describe an assembly by applying additional information such as a description, copyright, company name, and so on. This information is stored in the assembly manifest and displayed by various tools such as Windows Explorer, Visual Studio .NET, and ILDasm.

Assembly attributes come in two categories:

- **General informational attributes**: These assembly attributes exist only to record supplemental information, such as a copyright, company name, and description.

- **Informational and behavioral attributes**: These assembly attributes record information regarding the assembly and affect the behavior of the runtime and compiler.

The following sections present examples of each of these assembly attribute types.

General Informational Assembly Attributes

The use of informational assembly attributes is straightforward. Simply apply the attribute to the assembly (usually in the AssemblyInfo.cs file), and the compiler will add the information to the assembly manifest. Tools such as Windows Explorer and Visual Studio .NET can retrieve the information from the manifest as required.

For example, the code in Listing 2-7 uses various assembly attributes to specify an assembly description, company name, and product name.

Listing 2-7. Applying Some Assembly Attributes

```
using System.Reflection;   // Contains the assembly attributes

[assembly: AssemblyTitle("Assembly Attributes Demostration")]
[assembly: AssemblyDescription("This assembly demonstrates various " +
                               "assembly attributes")]
[assembly: AssemblyCompany("B&B Enterprises")]
[assembly: AssemblyProduct(".NET Attributes")]
[assembly: AssemblyCopyright("2003")]
[assembly: AssemblyFileVersion("1.0.0.0")]
[assembly: AssemblyInformationalVersion("2.0.0.0")]
```

When this example is compiled, the information is saved in the assembly manifest. You can view the results in ILDasm, as shown in Figure 2-5.

```
MANIFEST
.assembly TestLibrary
{
  .custom instance void [mscorlib]System.Reflection.AssemblyInformationalVersionAttribute::.ctor(str
  .custom instance void [mscorlib]System.Reflection.AssemblyFileVersionAttribute::.ctor(string) = (
  .custom instance void [mscorlib]System.Reflection.AssemblyCopyrightAttribute::.ctor(string) = ( 01
  .custom instance void [mscorlib]System.Reflection.AssemblyProductAttribute::.ctor(string) = ( 01 0
                                                                                                65 7
  .custom instance void [mscorlib]System.Reflection.AssemblyCompanyAttribute::.ctor(string) = ( 01 0
                                                                                                65 7
  .custom instance void [mscorlib]System.Reflection.AssemblyDescriptionAttribute::.ctor(string) = (


  .custom instance void [mscorlib]System.Reflection.AssemblyTitleAttribute::.ctor(string) = ( 01 00
                                                                                              69 62
                                                                                              69 6F
```

Figure 2-5. The assembly attributes as recorded in the manifest

You can also see this information using Windows Explorer by right-clicking the assembly and selecting Properties from the context menu. Figure 2-6 shows an example of viewing assembly information in Windows Explorer.

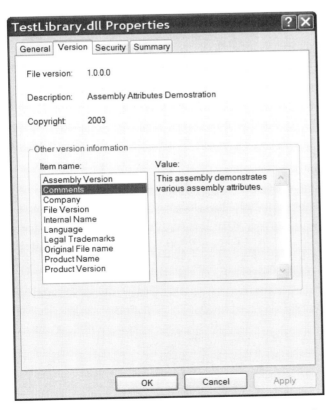

Figure 2-6. The assembly information shown in Windows Explorer

Informational and Behavioral Assembly Attributes

In addition to the general information assembly attributes, the .NET Framework also provides several attributes that not only describe the assembly, but also affect the behavior of the compiler or the runtime. These include the AssemblyKeyFile, AssemblyDelaySign, and AssemblyVersion attributes.

Using Attributes to Create Strong-Named Assemblies

With the AssemblyKeyFile attribute, you can direct the compiler to a file containing a public/private key pair. The compiler uses these keys to create a *strong-named assembly*. Strong-named assemblies have a few advantages over regular assemblies:

- When loading a strong-named assembly, the runtime takes extra steps to verify that it has not been modified from its original compiled state to do something malicious like spawn a virus or steal passwords.

- The runtime verifies the version number of strong-named assemblies, ensuring that a client application loads only the version of the assembly it was built against.

- A strong-named assembly can be shared across multiple applications by installing the assembly in the Global Assembly Cache (GAC).

To generate a strong-named assembly, the compiler[1] first hashes the contents of the assembly into a few hundred bytes. It then encrypts these bytes using the private key from the key file specified in the AssemblyKeyFile attribute to yield the assembly's digital signature. The digital signature is then stored within the assembly, and the public key (also from the specified key file) is saved within the assembly manifest. When the runtime loads the assembly into memory (or when the assembly is installed in the GAC), it decrypts the digital signature using the public key from the manifest to retrieve the compile-time hash. Then the runtime hashes the assembly again and compares this new hash against the compile-time hash. If the hashes match, the runtime has confirmed that the assembly has not been altered since it was compiled.

Of course, this entire process assumes that you have generated a key file containing a public/private key pair. Fortunately, the .NET Framework ships with a command-line utility, sn.exe, that randomly generates a public/private key pair and places them in a key file. The sn tool has a variety of options. As an example, Figure 2-7 demonstrates how to use the –k option to generate a key file.

---

1. Technically speaking, the linker actually performs the steps to generate the strong-named assembly. But most developers identify more with the compiler terminology.

```
C:\WINDOWS\System32\cmd.exe                                         _ □ ×

D:\>sn -k mykey.snk

Microsoft (R) .NET Framework Strong Name Utility  Version 1.0.3705.0
Copyright (C) Microsoft Corporation 1998-2001. All rights reserved.

Key pair written to mykey.snk

D:\>
```

Figure 2-7. Generating a key file with the sn utility

Once you have generated the key file, simply apply the AssemblyKeyFile attribute and pass the path to the key file into its constructor, like this:

```
[assembly: AssemblyKeyFile(@"d:\mykey.snk")]
```

 NOTE *If you specify a relative path in the* AssemblyKeyFile *attribute, the path is evaluated from the obj\debug subdirectory of your project directory.*

The next time you build the project, the compiler will use the key file to produce a strong-named assembly. A quick way to confirm that the assembly has a strong-name is to view the manifest using ILDasm and verify that it contains a public key. As noted earlier, every strong-named assembly has a public key in its manifest, as shown in Figure 2-8.

```
MANIFEST                                                          _ □ X
.assembly TestLibrary
{
  .custom instance void [mscorlib]System.Reflection.AssemblyKeyFileAttribute::.ctor

  // --- The following custom attribute is added automatically, do not uncomment --
  //   .custom instance void [mscorlib]System.Diagnostics.DebuggableAttribute::.ctor
  //
  .publickey = (00 24 00 00 04 80 00 00 94 00 00 00 06 02 00 00   // .$............
                00 24 00 00 52 53 41 31 00 04 00 00 01 00 01 00   // .$..RSA1......
                37 F1 67 6A 67 FB EA EF 02 1E 8B 15 9F 53 8C 59   // 7.gjg........s
                7C 39 02 D8 D1 B3 82 66 65 4E 2D 90 08 AB 9F 87   // |9.....feN-...
                71 5D 6C 9F 44 76 78 27 0A 2D 9C 21 76 2E 22 3D   // q]l.Dvx'.-.!v.
                20 E1 59 C0 5E 38 82 49 54 A8 E8 32 79 E2 D6 AA   // .Y.^8.IT..2y.
                76 03 84 74 C6 3C AF AE 08 6E E3 D5 EE 4A 3E 10   // v..t.<...n...(
                A9 9C 71 9A D9 70 94 9C C6 ED 85 ED 40 F1 13 3B   // ..q..p......@.
                B3 88 BD 51 98 C8 8C 64 D0 B3 1E 61 10 BC 73 FF   // ...Q...d...a..
                38 FA D6 D8 62 5A B8 1A EE 3D 4C C4 0B 30 6D FA )  // 8...bZ...=L..(
  .hash algorithm 0x00008004
  .ver 1:0:1241:6797
}
```

Figure 2-8. *The public key is stored in the assembly manifest*

Using Delayed Signing

The AssemblyKeyFile attribute makes creating strong-named assemblies easy, but there is one drawback: all developers must have access to both the public and private keys in the key file. The private key, however, is a very sensitive item. With it, a hacker or disgruntled employee can deploy malicious assemblies to your customers. Because these assemblies are signed using the stolen private key, the runtime will treat them as if they came from your organization. For this reason, an organization may wish to avoid distributing the key file even to its own developers. On the other hand, for testing purposes, developers need to re-create the actual deployment environment as closely as possible. Therefore, if an assembly is intended to be shared, it is best developed and tested in that manner early in the development process.

The solution to this dilemma is to use the AssemblyDelaySign attribute to enable *delayed signing*. With delayed signing enabled, the compiler requires only the public key, which it saves in the assembly manifest to generate a pseudo strong-named assembly. Other assemblies built against this delayed-signed assembly will treat it like a normal strong-named assembly, thus providing a realistic development and test environment. When the application is ready for deployment, the developers responsible for maintaining the organization's private key can use that key to give real strong-names to the assemblies.

To enable delayed signing, the first step is to retrieve only the public key from the key file. The sn tool provides the –p option for this purpose. For example, the following command retrieves the public key from the MyKey.snk file and saves it in the MyPublicKey.snk file:

```
sn -p MyKey.snk MyPublicKey.snk
```

The public key file can now be freely distributed to all developers for delayed signing.

To delay-sign an assembly, you apply both the `AssemblyKeyFile` and `AssemblyDelaySign` attributes, as shown in the following example:

```
// Tell compiler to use delayed signing
[assembly: AssemblyDelaySign(true)]

// Specify the location of the public key
[assembly: AssemblyKeyFile(@"D:\MyPublicKey.snk")]
```

Notice that the `AssemblyKeyFile` attribute no longer specifies the file containing the full key pair. Instead, it specifies the file containing only the public key.

The final step is to turn off the normal signature-verification process that occurs whenever a strong-named assembly is installed in the GAC or loaded by a client at runtime. The sn utility provides this functionality with the –Vr option, which allows you to register a given assembly for verification skipping. The following command registers the TestLibrary.dll for verification skipping on the current machine:

```
sn -Vr TestLibrary.dll
```

To unregister the assembly and reenable verification, use the –Vu option, as follows:

```
sn -Vu TestLibrary.dll
```

After the application is complete, you must sign the delayed-signed assemblies with the private key before deploying them to customers. As you can probably guess, the sn utility also provides this functionality, with its –R option. For example, the following command gives the TestLibrary.dll a real strong-name using the keys found in the MyKey.snk file:

```
sn -R TestLibrary.dll d:\MyKey.snk
```

Using the AssemblyVersion Attribute

As noted earlier, strong-named assemblies are strictly versioned. Without any further input, the runtime will load a strong-named assembly only if a client explicitly requests the correct version. This implies that you can assign a version number to an assembly, which is precisely the purpose of the `AssemblyVersion` attribute.

An assembly's version is described by a four-part version number stored in the manifest. The four parts are named major version, minor version, build number, and revision, respectively. They are delimited with either a period (.) or colon (:).

```
<major>.<minor>.<build>.<revision>
```

When you create a new project, Visual Studio .NET automatically adds the following line to the AssemblyInfo.cs file:

```
[assembly: AssemblyVersion("1.0.*")]
```

This use of the `AssemblyVersion` attribute sets the major version value to 1 and the minor version value to 0. The asterisk (*) in place of the build number and revision values tells the compiler to automatically generate these values each time the assembly is built. However, you can also explicitly set the version number, as shown in the following example:

```
[assembly: AssemblyVersion("2.0.1.1")]
```

Figure 2-9 shows how this version information is recorded in the assembly's manifest.

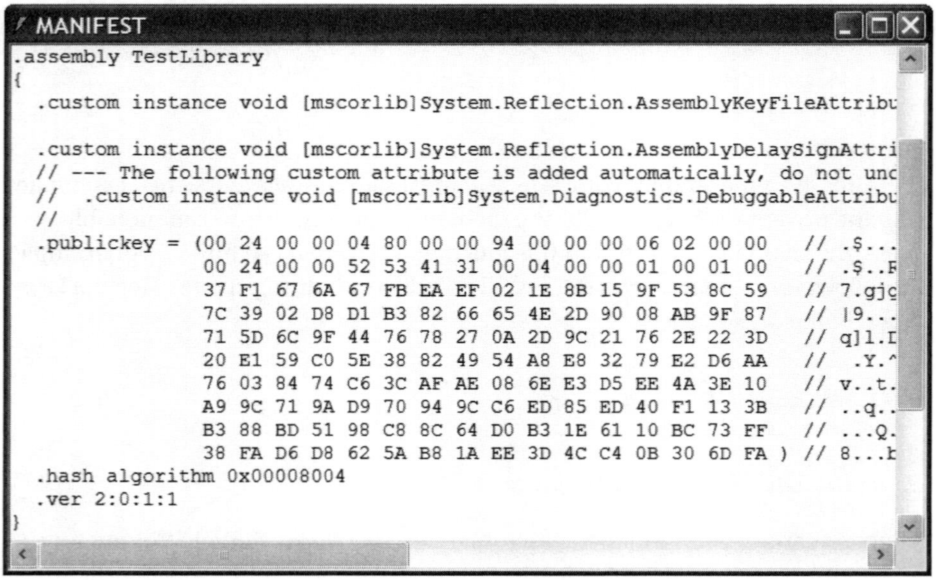

Figure 2-9. The version number is stored in the assembly manifest

When a client that references this assembly is compiled, the compiler records the assembly's version number in the client's manifest. This allows the client to request the correct version of the assembly at runtime. Figure 2-10 shows an example of an assembly version number recorded in a client's manifest.

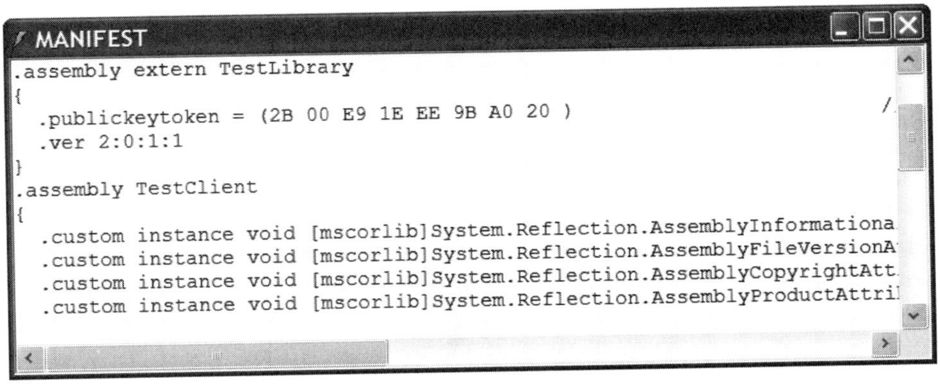

Figure 2-10. The assembly version number is also recorded in each client's manifest

COM Interoperability Attributes

.NET is a replacement for Microsoft's older COM technology. However, after nine years of touting the benefits of COM, Microsoft could not leave its customers with millions of dollars invested in worthless code. So as .NET was being developed, its developers took steps to ensure that it could leverage existing COM code. The resulting functionality is collectively known as the COM interoperability services (henceforth shortened to COM interop).

COM interop works in two directions:

- .NET code can call COM code using a Runtime Callable Wrapper (RCW).

- COM code can call into .NET code using a COM Callable Wrapper (CCW).

Both of these wrappers can be generated automatically using tools provided in the .NET Framework, such as regasm, tlbimp, and tlbexp.

Of the two directions, the most frequently used is the former, .NET code calling COM code. This is primarily due to the relatively early adoption of ASP.NET. Although companies are porting their COM-based Active Server Pages (ASP) Web pages to ASP.NET, many are choosing to retain their COM-based business objects or are slowly porting these to .NET as time and funds allow. However, the .NET-to-COM direction of interop does not make heavy use of attributes, and those it does use are runtime attributes. So this section focuses on the opposite direction: COM code calling .NET code. In Chapter 3, you will learn about *platform invoke* and the attributes that are used for .NET code calling into COM code.

The .NET Framework provides several attributes to help your .NET classes integrate more easily with the world of COM. For the most part, these COM interop attributes control the behavior of various .NET Framework tools including tlbexp, regasm, and regsvcs. These tools can read a specified .NET assembly and generate, and optionally register, a corresponding COM type library.

Surveying the Interop Issues

The COM and .NET runtimes are extremely different. This leads to several issues that you must overcome in order to expose .NET classes to the COM universe. Table 2-1 summarizes these issues.

Table 2-1. COM and .NET Runtime Differences

Issue	COM	.NET
Locating dynamic link libraries (DLLs)	Uses the system registry to look up the location of a requested COM DLL.	Uses the assembly binding mechanism, which includes a search heuristic for locating a requested assembly. This does not require a registration step.
Lifetime	The lifetime of a COM object is determined via reference counting. Basically, every reference to the object is counted, and when the reference count goes to zero, the object is destroyed.	Uses garbage collection.
Type system	The COM type system is loosely based on variant compliant types.	.NET types strictly conform to a more robust set of types defined in the CTS.

Table 2-1. COM and .NET Runtime Differences (continued)

Issue	COM	.NET
Type identification	Uses globally unique identifiers (GUIDs) extensively to identify classes, interfaces, type libraries, and more.	Uses the assembly name, namespace, and type name to identify types. The assembly name can include strong-named information, in which case the assembly version and public key help identify types.
Versioning	COM also uses GUIDs to facilitate versioning. Developers (or their tools) must apply a new GUID to any modified class or interface.	Handles versioning via the assembly's version number.
Referencing objects	COM is purely interfaced-based, meaning that any reference to an object is really pointing to an interface, not the entire object.	.NET references can point to either an interface or the entire object.

As the upcoming sections show, overcoming these differences requires a mixture of tools and, of course, attributes.

Registering Assemblies for COM Interop

The first issue listed in Table 2-1, locating DLLs, is handled by a tool called regasm. This tool reads a given assembly, generates a corresponding COM type library, and registers the type library. Once this is done, any COM client can use the types defined in the .NET assembly. From the COM client's perspective, the process of finding the DLL, loading the DLL, and using the contained types is exactly the same as with any other COM DLL. The fact that the COM client is actually calling a .NET assembly is completely hidden from the client.

Regasm is also responsible for generating the COM-visible portion of the COM CCW. At runtime, the CCW handles the interaction between the COM client and the .NET object by exposing a COM-friendly interface to the COM client. The CCW automatically converts COM types into their .NET counterparts and vice versa. It also maps COM's reference-counting mechanism to .NET's garbage-collection scheme. In other words, the CCW resolves the type system and lifetime issues noted in Table 2-1.

The regasm tool provides many options, but the following example demonstrates a typical use of this tool:

```
regasm -tlb:TestLibrary.tlb TestLibrary.dll
```

This example instructs regasm to read the TestLibrary.dll (a .NET assembly) and generate a corresponding COM type library named TestLibrary.tlb. It also registers the type library on the current machine. At this point, a COM client application can reference and use the type library in the same way that it would use any other COM type library. However, in reality, the COM runtime loads the .NET assembly into the COM client's process. Any method calls made on the types in the type library are passed to the .NET assembly for execution.

Developing for COM Interop

So far, we have not mentioned any attributes related to COM interop, just the regasm tool and the CCW. However, there are still a number of issues left to resolve: type identification, versioning, and referencing objects. These are issues that you must overcome by applying .NET attributes.

COM interop attributes change the behavior of the regasm tool while it processes the assembly and affects how it generates the corresponding type library. In effect, COM interop attributes allow you to control exactly how your .NET objects are exposed to COM clients, which allows you to work around some of the interoperability issues.

The ClassInterface Attribute

One interoperability issue concerns how to expose members of a .NET class to COM. Since COM is purely an interface-based system, it cannot directly access the members of a class. By default, the type library generated by regasm exposes class members using the COM IDispatch interface, which is COM's mechanism for late binding. Therefore, unless you specify otherwise, COM clients can only late-bind to the .NET object. This means that method calls cannot be validated at compiler-time and also results in far slower performance as compared to early binding.

For example, consider the code in Listing 2-8. This code defines a `SimpleMath` class that will be used in the following examples to demonstrate the effects of COM interop attributes. Assume that this code is compiled into a MathLibrary.dll assembly.

Listing 2-8. The SimpleMath Class Defined Within MathLibrary.dll

```
public class SimpleMath
{
    public int Add(int n1, int n2)
    {
        return n1 + n2;
    }
    public int Subtract(int n1, int n2)
    {
        return n1 - n2;
    }
}
```

When you export this `SimpleMath` class to COM using regasm, it creates the COM coclass shown in Listing 2-9.

Listing 2-9. The SimpleMath Coclass in the Generated Type Library

```
coclass SimpleMath {
    [default] interface _SimpleMath;
    interface _Object;
};

interface _SimpleMath : IDispatch {
};
```

Note that the `SimpleMath` coclass defines a default interface named `_SimpleMath`. This interface is called the *class interface* because it represents the `SimpleMath` class and provides access to all of its members. However, the class interface defined in Listing 2-9 derives from `IDispatch` and does not contain any information regarding the `Add` or `Subtract` methods. Therefore, COM clients can only late-bind to the `SimpleMath` class.

To fully appreciate the issues related to this, let's assume that we wish to create a Visual Basic 6 (VB6) COM client that consumes the MathLibrary assembly. In this case, we simply set a reference to the generated COM type library (MathLibrary.tlb). However, when we view the `SimpleMath` class in the VB6 Object Browser, it does not display any members, as shown in Figure 2-11.

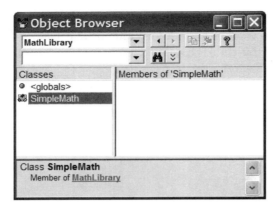

Figure 2-11. The VB6 Object Browser does not display members of the SimpleMath class

More important, this means that the VB6 compiler cannot catch incorrect calls to the SimpleMath methods. For example, consider the VB6 code in Listing 2-10.

Listing 2-10. Calling (Incorrectly) the SimpleMath.Add() Method from VB6

```
Private Sub btnAdd_Click()
    Dim math As SimpleMath
    Set math = CreateObject("MathLibrary.SimpleMath")

    'Invoke SimpleMath.Add with wrong number of arguments!
    MsgBox math.Add(5)
End Sub
```

Although this example calls the Add() method with one argument instead of two, it compiles without error. We would not get an error until runtime.

To fix this problem, we can apply the ClassInterface attribute. This attribute accepts a ClassInterfaceType enumeration that allows you to specify exactly how regasm should generate the class interface. Table 2-2 lists the members of the ClassInterfaceType and how each affects the generated type library.

Table 2-2. The ClassInterfaceType Members

ClassInterfaceType Member	Description
AutoDispatch	This is the default behavior. Regasm generates a late-bound-only class interface, as shown in Listing 2-9.
AutoDual	With this setting, regasm generates a dual-interface class interface that includes all public class members and inherited members.
None	With this setting, regasm does not generate a class interface. Therefore, COM clients can access only interface members implemented by the class.

For example, the code in Listing 2-11 applies the ClassInterface attribute and specifies the AutoDual setting.

Listing 2-11. Applying the ClassInterface Attribute with the AutoDual Setting

```
using System.Runtime.InteropServices;   // contains interop types

[ClassInterface(ClassInterfaceType.AutoDual)]
public class SimpleMath
{
    public int Add(int n1, int n2)
    {
        return n1 + n2;
    }
    public int Subtract(int n1, int n2)
    {
        return n1 - n2;
    }
}
```

When regasm processes this code, it generates the SimpleMath coclass shown in Listing 2-12.

Listing 2-12. The SimpleMath Coclass with AutoDual Specified

```
coclass SimpleMath {
    [default] interface _SimpleMath;
    interface _Object;
};
```

```
interface _SimpleMath : IDispatch {
    [id(00000000), propget, custom(54FC8F55-38DE-4703-9C4E-250351302B1C, 1)]
    HRESULT ToString([out, retval] BSTR* pRetVal);
    [id(0x60020001)]
    HRESULT Equals(
                    [in] VARIANT obj,
                    [out, retval] VARIANT_BOOL* pRetVal);
    [id(0x60020002)]
    HRESULT GetHashCode([out, retval] long* pRetVal);
    [id(0x60020003)]
    HRESULT GetType([out, retval] _Type** pRetVal);

    [id(0x60020004)]
    HRESULT Add(
                [in] long n1,
                [in] long n2,
                [out, retval] long* pRetVal);
    [id(0x60020005)]
    HRESULT Subtract(
                [in] long n1,
                [in] long n2,
                [out, retval] long* pRetVal);
};
```

As Listing 2-12 shows, the _SimpleMath interface now includes the Add() and Subtract() methods. It also includes methods inherited from System.Object: Equals(), GetHashCode(), ToString(), and so on. In fact, when you apply the AutoDual setting, regasm includes all public class members in the default interface, including those inherited from all base classes.

This updated type library allows COM clients to early-bind to the SimpleMath class. For example, now the VB6 code in Listing 2-10 will not compile. Also the VB6 Object Browser displays all of the _SimpleMath members, as shown in Figure 2-12.

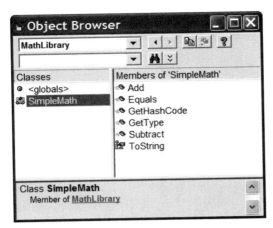

Figure 2-12. With the AutoDual setting applied, the VB6 Object Browser displays all the public SimpleMath *members, including inherited members*

.NET Interfaces for COM Interop

Although the AutoDual setting is an easy way to provide early binding to COM clients, the preferred technique is to interoperate with COM clients exclusively through .NET interfaces. In other words, the class public members should be members of an implemented interface. This provides more robust versioning and follows COM's notion of pure interface-based programming.

For example, the code in Listing 2-13 modifies the original SimpleMath class definition by defining and implementing an ISimpleMath interface.

Listing 2-13. Using Interfaces and the ClassInterfaceType.None Setting

```
public interface ISimpleMath
{
    int Add(int n1, int n2);
    int Subtract(int n1, int n2);
}

[ClassInterface(ClassInterfaceType.None)]
public class SimpleMath : ISimpleMath
{
    public int Add(int n1, int n2)
    {
        return n1 + n2;
    }
```

```
    public int Subtract(int n1, int n2)
    {
        return n1 - n2;
    }
}
```

This example applies the ClassInterfaceType.None setting. In this case, regasm does *not* generate a class interface. Instead, it generates a COM interface for each implemented interface. It also creates a coclass that implements these interfaces. If you run regasm against the SimpleMath class in Listing 2-13, it produces the type library definitions shown in Listing 2-14.

Listing 2-14. The SimpleMath Coclass with the ClassInterfaceType.None Setting

```
coclass SimpleMath {
    interface _Object;
    [default] interface ISimpleMath;
};

interface ISimpleMath : IDispatch {
    [id(0x60020000)]
    HRESULT Add(
                [in] long n1,
                [in] long n2,
                [out, retval] long* pRetVal);
    [id(0x60020001)]
    HRESULT Subtract(
                [in] long n1,
                [in] long n2,
                [out, retval] long* pRetVal);
};
```

This example begins to demonstrate why interfaces are the preferred way to expose functionality to COM clients. Instead of exposing all of the public class members and inherited members, the ISimpleMath interface exposes only the Add() and Subtract() methods. Also, because this interface is marked as the default interface, when a COM client creates a SimpleMath object, it will receive a reference to the ISimpleMath interface and therefore will be able to invoke only Add() or Subtract().

NOTE *If a .NET class implements multiple interfaces, regasm configures the first interface listed as the default interface.*

Figure 2-13 shows how the VB6 Object Browser displays the `SimpleMath` class after the `ClassInterfaceType.None` setting is applied. Notice that it now displays only the `Add()` and `Subtract()` methods.

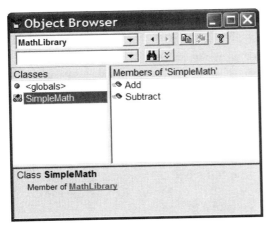

Figure 2-13. With ClassInterfaceType.None applied, the VB6 Object Browser displays only the ISimpleMath members

In addition to applying the `ClassInterface` attribute to each individual class, you can also apply it to the assembly. Therefore, if you wish to use the interface technique to expose every class in the assembly to COM clients, you can enter the following line of code in the AssemblyInfo.cs file.

```
[assembly: ClassInterface(ClassInterfaceType.None)]
```

NOTE   *If the* `ClassInterfaceType.None` *setting is applied to a class that does not implement an interface, the* `_Object` *interface is used as the class interface. This interface contains only the* `System.Object` *methods and therefore is not particularly useful from a COM client's perspective.*

Identity, Versioning, and the Guid Attribute

COM uses a 128-bit number as a GUID to identify items in a type library and to facilitate versioning. When you compile an early-bound COM client, it embeds the GUIDs within the corresponding executable. At runtime, the client passes these GUIDs to the COM runtime, which uses them to find and activate the requested types. Therefore, if a GUID changes in a type library, any early-bound clients built against the old GUID are broken.

When generating a type library for COM interop, the regasm tool must also generate and apply GUIDs to the contained items. Exactly how regasm generates the GUID depends on the item it will identify.

- To generate a GUID identifying the type library (TLBID), regasm hashes the assembly's friendly name (for example, MathLibrary) and version. If the assembly is strong-named, then the strong-name is hashed to generate the TLBID.

- To generate a GUID identifying a class (CLSID), regasm hashes the full class name (including the namespace) and the assembly version.

- To generate a GUID identifying an interface (IID), regasm hashes the interface name and the signatures of all its members. Reordering the members within the interface results in a different IID.

You can override this default regasm behavior by applying the Guid attribute to an assembly, class, or interface. When this attribute is present, regasm uses the provided GUID to identify the item, instead of generating a GUID. For example, the code in Listing 2-15 uses the Guid attribute to manually assign a GUID to the ISimpleMath interface.

Listing 2-15. Applying the Guid Attribute

```
[Guid("6FE58D52-36BC-4a83-9258-004C5805B9EA")]
public interface ISimpleMath
{
    int Add(int n1, int n2);
    int Subtract(int n1, int n2);
}


[ClassInterface(ClassInterfaceType.None)]
public class SimpleMath : ISimpleMath
{
    public int Add(int n1, int n2)
    {
        return n1 + n2;
    }
    public int Subtract(int n1, int n2)
    {
        return n1 - n2;
    }
}
```

In the generated type library, the ISimpleMath interface is now represented as follows:

```
[
    odl,
    uuid(6FE58D52-36BC-4A83-9258-004C5805B9EA),
    version(1.0),
    dual,
    oleautomation,
    custom(0F21F359-AB84-41E8-9A78-36D110E6D2F9, MathLibrary.ISimpleMath)
]
interface ISimpleMath : IDispatch {
    // Snip ...
};
```

In this type library excerpt, notice that the uuid value is identical to the one provided in the Guid attribute in Listing 2-15.

 TIP   *To generate a unique GUID to apply via the Guid attribute, you can use the uuidgen.exe command-line tool or Visual Studio .NET. In Visual Studio .NET, select Tools ➤ Create GUID, and then copy and paste the resulting GUID into your code.*

Listing 2-16 demonstrates another reason why the interface approach is preferred over the ClassInterfaceType.AutoDual setting. With the AutoDual setting, regasm automatically generates the interface and the IID. As a result, if you add methods to the class, regasm will generate a new IID and break early-bound clients. However, by using an interface and manually applying the IID, you can add methods without breaking existing clients. You can even change method signatures by defining the new methods in a different interface. This leaves the existing interface and its method intact for backward compatibility with existing clients. Newly developed clients, on the other hand, can choose to call the updated method in the new interface.

As an example, Listing 2-16 defines "new and improved" Add() and Subtract() methods that accept three integers instead of two. To avoid breaking existing COM clients that use the two-integer version of Add(), the new methods are defined in a new interface named ISimpleMath2.

Listing 2-16. Versioning Using Interfaces and the Guid Attribute

```
[Guid("6FE58D52-36BC-4a83-9258-004C5805B9EA")]
public interface ISimpleMath
{
    int Add(int n1, int n2);
    int Subtract(int n1, int n2);
}


[Guid("C3566746-B13B-4fcc-9E40-446A4C183CDA")]
public interface ISimpleMath2
{
    int Add(int n1, int n2, int n3);
    int Subtract(int n1, int n2, int n3);
}


[ClassInterface(ClassInterfaceType.None)]
public class SimpleMath : ISimpleMath, ISimpleMath2
{
    public int Add(int n1, int n2)
    {
        return n1 + n2;
    }
    public int Subtract(int n1, int n2)
    {
        return n1 - n2;
    }
    public int Add(int n1, int n2, int n3)
    {
        return n1 + n2 + n3;
    }
    public int Subtract(int n1, int n2, int n3)
    {
        return n1 - n2 - n3;
    }
}
```

Other COM Interop Tools

Although the previous sections have focused on COM interop with the regasm tool, that is not the only .NET Framework tool that can generate COM type libraries. The .NET Framework also provides tlbexp and regsvcs.

Tlbexp behaves in the same way as regasm, except that it does not register the generated type library. Because regasm does register the type library, it is a bit more convenient to use.

Regsvcs is used to register serviced components. Like regasm, it also generates and registers COM type libraries. Chapter 3 discusses the regsvcs utility in more detail.

Regardless of the tool you use, the COM interop attributes described in the previous section have the same effect on the resulting type library.

Design-time Attributes

Command-line utilities like regasm and regsvcs are not the only tools that read and respond to attributes. In fact, some attributes control the behavior of Visual Studio .NET. When you apply these attributes to a custom user interface control, for example, they allow that control to integrate into Visual Studio .NET in the same way as a built-in control. Since these attributes affect how you configure the control at design-time, they are called *design-time attributes*.

Creating a Simple Control

Compared to previous technologies, Visual Studio .NET makes creating custom user interface controls extremely easy. In many cases, all you need to do is create a Windows control library project in Visual Studio .NET. The resulting project contains an initial class that derives from the UserControl class. You can then use the control designer to create the look and feel of the control, similar to how you use it when creating a form. For example, Listing 2-17 shows a simple custom control named MyLabelControl. This is a custom constituent control that wraps a standard Label control.

Listing 2-17. Defining a Custom Control Class

```
public class MyLabelControl : UserControl
{
    private const string DEFAULT_MESSAGE = "My custom label control";
    private System.Windows.Forms.Label lblMessage;

    public string Message
    {
        get { return lblMessage.Text; }
        set { lblMessage.Text = value; }
    }
}
```

```
    private void MyLabelControl_Load(object sender, System.EventArgs e)
    {
        lblMessage.Text = DEFAULT_MESSAGE;
    }
    // Component Designer generated code ...
}
```

Figure 2-14 shows the visual portion of this custom control in the designer.

Figure 2-14. MyLabelControl in the Visual Studio .NET designer

Notice that this control class exposes a public Message property that allows the user interface (UI) developer to specify the text to display in the label. When this control is placed on a form at design-time, Visual Studio .NET automatically adds the Message property to the Properties window, as shown in Figure 2-15.

Figure 2-15. Visual Studio .NET automatically includes custom properties in the Properties window

Applying Design-time Attributes to the Control

If you take a closer look at Figure 2-15, you will notice a couple of undesirable factors. First, the Message property appears as the last property under the Misc category. Second, the Properties window typically displays a helpful description of the selected property. However, with the Message property selected, it displays nothing.

Fortunately, the System.ComponentModel namespace contains several attributes that you can use to configure how a custom property appears in the Properties window. These attributes are described in Table 2-3.

Table 2-3. Design-time Attributes

Attribute	Description
AmbientValue	Marks an ambient property, which is a property that queries the control's host for its value.
Bindable	Applies to a property that is typically used for binding and raises a property change event.
Browsable	Controls whether a property is displayed in the Properties window.
Category	Specifies that a property belongs to the given category.
DefaultEvent	Specifies the default event for a component. This event will be assumed when the component is double-clicked from the designer.
DefaultProperty	Specifies the default property for a component.
DefaultValue	Specifies the default value for a property. Used to reset the property.
Description	Specifies the description of the property to be displayed in the Properties window.
DesignOnly	Specifies that the property can be set only at design-time.
Editor	Associates an editor with a property. This is helpful when the property cannot be edited easily with a simple text box as provided in the Properties window.
ListBindable	Specifies that the property can be bound to a list.
ParenthesizePropertyName	Indicates that the Properties window should display the property name in parentheses. Parenthesized properties appear at the top of the list.
ToolBoxBitmap	Part of the System.Drawing namespace. Specifies the bitmap used to represent a control in the ToolBox.

Listing 2-18 shows several of the attributes in the System.ComponentModel namespace applied to the MyLabelControl.Message property.

Listing 2-18. Applying Design-time Attributes to the Message Property

```
public class MyLabelControl : UserControl
{
    private const string DEFAULT_MESSAGE = "My custom label control";
    private System.Windows.Forms.Label lblMessage;

    [DefaultValue(DEFAULT_MESSAGE)]
    [Category("My Custom Properties")]
    [Description("The message displayed in the control")]
    [ParenthesizePropertyName(true)]
    public string Message
    {
        get { return lblMessage.Text; }
        set { lblMessage.Text = value; }
    }

    private void MyLabelControl_Load(object sender, System.EventArgs e)
    {
        lblMessage.Text = DEFAULT_MESSAGE;
    }

    // Component Designer generated code ...
}
```

As you can see in Figure 2-16, these attributes change several aspects of the Properties window's display. First, the Message property now appears under the My Custom Properties category. Second, the property name is in parentheses, which means that it will appear toward the top of the property list when displayed in alphabetical order rather than by category. Finally, the Properties window displays the provided description when the Message property is selected.

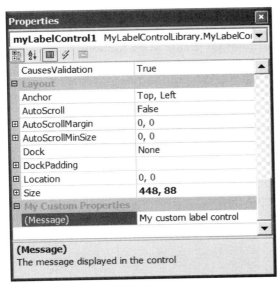

Figure 2-16. The Message property with design-time attributes applied

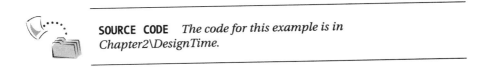

SOURCE CODE *The code for this example is in Chapter2\DesignTime.*

Conclusion

Although .NET attributes typically affect runtime behavior, this chapter has introduced several attributes that modify compiler or tool behavior and demonstrated how to use them. You have learned the following about compile-time and design-time attributes:

- How to create conditional methods using the Conditional attribute

- How to force the compiler to check for or ignore CLS-compliance issues in your code

- How to specify general information regarding an assembly, such as your company name, assembly description, and copyright

- How to create a strong-named assembly with delayed signing

- How to apply COM interop attributes to create COM-friendly .NET classes

- How to apply design-time attributes to custom controls for better integration with the Visual Studio .NET integrated development environment (IDE)

In the next chapter, you'll learn about attributes that affect the behavior of the runtime. And while compile-time attributes are certainly useful, you will see that runtime attributes provide a huge set of functionality, ranging from security, to serialization, to integrating with COM+.

CHAPTER 3

Attributes and Runtime Behavior

As you saw in Chapter 2, you can use attributes to alter the outcome of the compilation process. But that is not the only time attributes come into play. Some attributes are examined as the code is running, and their presence in the assembly results in certain actions. For example, security-based attributes can be used to state that certain permissions must exist; otherwise, the code will not execute. Other attributes allow an object's state to be persisted to disk. This chapter will cover some of these runtime attributes and how they affect your code as it executes. We'll start our investigation of runtime attributes by looking at .NET security.

Securing Code

As you probably know by now, security is a major component of the .NET Framework. Not only is managed code verifiable by the runtime (so all sorts of nasty pointer problems can be identified before they occur), but you can also design your classes so that their code will execute only if the right permissions have been granted. Furthermore, users can configure the .NET runtime security layer to grant a specific set of permissions to a given assembly.

This section introduces the attribute-based aspect of .NET security. You'll learn how these attributes are added and how they affect your code's behavior at runtime. You'll see how using security-based attributes compares to implementing the security directly in the code. Finally, you'll discover where the security metadata is stored in the assembly and how you can extract it with a tool that comes with the .NET Framework.

Security in .NET

Essentially, the issue of security in .NET comes down to two features: permissions and evidence. The .NET runtime will determine if your code can do what it desires to do if it has enough information about the assembly (the evidence) to allow it (the permission) to invoke the action. Let's run through a brief example to see how this works. Listing 3-1 shows an example of how you can open a file in .NET and read through its data in binary mode in 100-byte chunks.

Listing 3-1. Opening a File in .NET

```
using System;
using System.IO;

public class FileOpener
{
    private const int CHUNK_SIZE = 100;

    public FileOpener() {}

    public int ReadFile(string filePath)
    {
        int retVal = 0;

        using(FileStream fs = File.Open(filePath, FileMode.Open,
                FileAccess.Read))
        {
            byte[] fileData = new byte[CHUNK_SIZE];
            int bytesRead = 0;

            while((bytesRead = fs.Read(
                fileData, 0, fileData.Length)) > 0)
            {
                // Do something wonderful with the file's data.
                retVal += bytesRead;
            }
        }

        return retVal;
    }
}
```

The code is fairly simple. All it does is read the information from the given file and then return the file size to the caller.[1] However, from a security standpoint, you can see where this code could be very dangerous. For example, the client could inadvertently pass in a file that has sensitive information, and

---

1. There is a much easier way to do this via the `Length` property on a `FileInfo` class, but the code's main purpose is to demonstrate security issues, not the most efficient way to read the size of a file.

FileOpener could easily read that information after Read() is called and the byte array is full of that information. Going the other way, the client could send a file to FileOpener that contains a virus. Depending on what FileOpener does with the file's contents, it could be in for a nasty surprise.

Fortunately, in .NET we have a number of ways to defend this code against malicious input. Let's add an attribute to deny FileOpener the ability to read information from the system directory.

```
[FileIOPermission(SecurityAction.Deny, Read=@"C:\Windows\System32")]
public int ReadFile(string filePath)
{
    //  Same code as before...
}
```

NOTE *If you're howling that the system directory we've used won't always have that value on every Windows machine, you're correct. Remember that any attribute must contain constant information in its values, so using* Environment.SystemDirectory *won't be allowed by the compiler. We'll take a look at an alternative approach to .NET security later in this chapter, in the "Declarative vs. Imperative Security" section.*

Now let's say that we have a WinForm client that uses FileOpener to open a file when a button is clicked via the following code:

```
private void btnReadFile_Click(object sender, System.EventArgs e)
{
    this.lblFileSizeValue.Text = string.Empty;

    string fileName = this.txtFileName.Text;

    if(fileName != null && fileName.Length > 0)
    {
        try
        {
            this.Cursor = Cursors.WaitCursor;
            FileOpener opener = new FileOpener();
            int fileSize = opener.ReadFile(fileName);
            this.lblFileSizeValue.Text = fileSize.ToString();
        }
        catch(Exception ex)
```

```
        {
            this.Cursor = Cursors.Default;
            MessageBox.Show(this, ex.Message,
                "File Opener Exception",
                MessageBoxButtons.OK,
                MessageBoxIcon.Exclamation);
        }
        finally
        {
            this.Cursor = Cursors.Default;
        }
    }
}
```

If the client entered C:\AccountInformation\SecretFinancialData.xls in the txtFileName text box, FileOpener wouldn't be stopped from reading that file.[2] However, trying to get FileOpener to read C:\Windows\System32\mscoree.dll would result in the message box shown in Figure 3-1 being displayed to the user.

Figure 3-1. Trying to read from an inaccessible file

There are a number of security-based attributes that you can use in your code, depending on which resource you want to lock down. All security attributes descend from SecurityAttribute, although it's more common for security attributes to descend from CodeAccessSecurityAttribute. Table 3-1 describes the security attributes that come with the .NET Framework.

---

2. Note that we're being very simplistic in this example. There are other ways to prevent FileOpener from reading a file than the attribute technique we showed here. For example, you could set up policies in .NET so that the assembly couldn't read the contents of that file.

Table 3-1. .NET Security Attributes

Attribute Name	Description
System.Data.Common.DBDataPermissionAttribute	Controls the aspects of database usage checks
System.Diagnostics.EventLogPermissionAttribute	Used for event log access checks
System.Diagnostics.PerformanceCounterPermissionAttribute	Determines accessibility to use performance counters
System.DirectoryServices.DirectoryServicesPermissionAttribute	Checks access to Active Directory information
System.Drawing.Printing.PrintingPermissionAttribute	Checks for permission to print
System.Messaging.MessageQueuePermissionAttribute	Used to verify valid Microsoft Message Queue (MSMQ) usage
System.Net.DnsPermissionAttribute	Checks the usage of a Domain Name Server (DNS)
System.Net.SocketPermissionAttribute	Controls socket resource usage
System.Net.WebPermissionAttribute	Verifies valid Web resource requests
System.Security.Permissions.EnvironmentPermissionAttribute	Used when environment information is requested
System.Security.Permissions.FileDialogPermissionAttribute	Verifies usage of a file dialog box
System.Security.Permissions.FileIOPermissionAttribute	Determines various file accessibility actions
System.Security.Permissions.IsolatedStoragePermissionAttribute	Checks for valid isolated storage usage
System.Security.Permissions.PermissionSetAttribute	Specifies a number of permissions that should be applied in the same fashion
System.Security.Permissions.PrincipalPermissionAttribute	Determines the accessibility of a resource via the membership of the AppDomain's identity to a role
System.Security.Permissions.PublisherIdentityPermissionAttribute	Allows access to a resource based on the identity's signature
System.Security.Permissions.ReflectionPermissionAttribute	Controls the usage of the Reflection API

Table 3-1. .NET Security Attributes (continued)

Attribute Name	Description
System.Security.Permissions. RegistryPermissionAttribute	Checks access to the registry
System.Security.Permissions. SecurityPermissionAttribute	Checks for access to general .NET facilities (such as configuring Remoted types and thread control)
System.Security.Permissions. SiteIdentityPermissionAttribute	Determines accessibility to URL-based resources based on the site's identity
System.Security.Permissions. StrongNameIdentityPermissionAttribute	Checks the strong-name to determine valid resource usage
System.Security.Permissions. UIPermissionAttribute	Performs various checks on UI resources
System.Security.Permissions. UrlIdentityPermissionAttribute	Checks for access to a fully specified URL
System.Security.Permissions. ZoneIdentityPermissionAttribute	Checks the current zone to determine resource accessibility
System.ServiceProcess. ServiceControllerPermissionAttribute	Determines if the caller can control a Windows service (WinService)

NOTE *It's possible to create your own custom security permission along with a related attribute. Refer to Chapter 4 of .NET Security by Jason Bock, Tom Fischer, Nathan Smith, and Pete Stromquist (Apress, 2002) for details on custom permissions as well as other security-related aspects of .NET.*

Each security attribute will have at least one constructor that takes a SecurityAction enumeration value. Table 3-2 lists these values, when they are checked, where they can be applied, and what they mean.

Table 3-2. SecurityAction Values

Value Name	Time of Verification	Valid Targets	Description
Assert	At runtime	Classes and methods	If the code has access to the resource, code higher in the stack does not need the permission.
Demand	At runtime	Classes and methods	Code higher in the stack must have this permission.
Deny	At runtime	Classes and methods	All downward code is denied access to the resource.
InheritanceDemand	At load-time	Classes and methods	Deriving classes must have access to the specified resource.
LinkDemand	At JIT-compilation	Classes and methods	Checks the immediate caller's accessibility *only*.
RequestMinimum	At grant-time	Assemblies	The assembly must have access to the specified resource to execute; it won't load if it doesn't.
RequestOptional	At grant-time	Assemblies	The assembly should have access to the specified resource to execute, but the assembly is still allowed to load if it doesn't.
RequestRefuse	At grant-time	Assemblies	The assembly will not have access to the specified resource during its execution.

To illustrate how these security attributes and actions determine how your code works, let's revisit our code that used FileIOPermissionAttribute. We used the Deny value to prevent FileOpener from reading any file from a given directory. However, using Demand *does not mean* your code can demand to get the permission to a resource; it only means that your code will immediately fail if it does not have the permissions to access the resource.

Let's dive a little deeper into the .NET Framework to show how this check works and where the security metadata comes into play. As you can probably glean from some of the descriptions of the SecurityAction values, these checks are stack-based. For example, suppose that method A calls method B, and method B calls method C, which has our FileIOPermissionAttribute attached to it with a Deny action on the System32 directory. In that case, method C and any methods that C calls will not have the permission to use files in that directory. To see what the runtime does to check for security-based attributes, we'll change the message box to show more information from the exception.

```
MessageBox.Show(this, ex.StackTrace, "File Opener Exception",
    MessageBoxButtons.OK,
    MessageBoxIcon.Exclamation);
```

Rather than display a huge stack trace in a message box, however, we'll show the stack trace in text form. We've also numbered the methods in the stack trace to make it easier to follow the code flow.

```
11) at System.Security.SecurityRuntime.FrameDescHelper(
      FrameSecurityDescriptor secDesc, IPermission demand,
      PermissionToken permToken)
10) at System.Security.CodeAccessSecurityEngine.Check(
      PermissionToken permToken, CodeAccessPermission demand,
      StackCrawlMark& stackMark, Int32 checkFrames,
      Int32 unrestrictedOverride)
9) at System.Security.CodeAccessSecurityEngine.Check(
      CodeAccessPermission cap, StackCrawlMark& stackMark)
8) at System.Security.CodeAccessPermission.Demand()
7) at System.IO.FileStream..ctor(String path, FileMode mode,
      FileAccess access, FileShare share, Int32 bufferSize,
      Boolean useAsync, String msgPath, Boolean bFromProxy)
6) at System.IO.FileStream..ctor(String path, FileMode mode,
      FileAccess access, FileShare share)
5) at System.IO.File.Open(String path, FileMode mode, FileAccess access,
      FileShare share)
4) at System.IO.File.Open(String path, FileMode mode, FileAccess access)
3) at FileOpener.ReadFile(String filePath)
2) at FileOpener.ReadFile(String filePath)
1) at FileOpenerClient.frmMain.btnReadFile_Click(Object sender,
      EventArgs e)
```

Figure 3-2 illustrates this call flow.

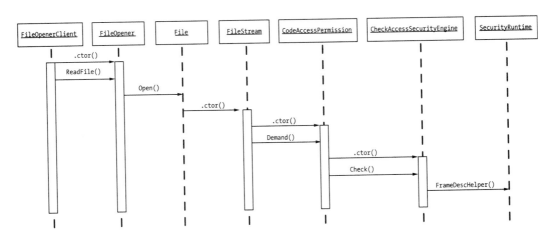

Figure 3-2. FileOpenerClient call stack

Let's start at the bottom of the stack. Our button's click event is fired, which we catch via btnReadFile_Click(). That uses FileOpener to read the contents of C:\Windows\System32\mscoree.dll. As you see at step 5, our call to File.Open() begins. This eventually leads to a call at step 8 to Demand(). As you'll learn in the "Declarative vs. Imperative Security" section later in this chapter, you can check for valid access to a resource without resorting to metadata, which is what the FileStream constructor is doing. This is extremely important point to notice, especially if you end up writing your own custom permission classes. Code that allows access to a resource *must* make a check to invoke the .NET security verification of the call stack. If FileStream's constructor didn't check its call stack, we would be able to read the contents of mscoree.dll.[3]

However, in our case, a stack check *is* made, which is where some internal .NET classes (such as System.Security.CodeAccessSecurityEngine and System.Security.SecurityRuntime) come into play. Two method calls—Check() and FrameDescHelper()—are used to look at a number of items related to security, one of which is the security-based metadata that exists.[4] In our case, we have a Deny action on ReadFile(). We're trying to read the contents of a file that is within the restricted directory, so our code fails.

---

3. We would still have one more hurdle to jump: the operating system's security layer. If .NET thinks it's okay for the file access to occur, but the process's identity doesn't have the right credentials, we would still get an exception.

4. Another aspect is the security configuration, which can also influence what an assembly can or cannot do. For more information, look up the ".NET Framework Configuration Tool" article in the SDK (ms-help://MS.NETFrameworkSDK/cptools/html/cpconnetframeworkadministrationtoolsmscorcfgmsc.htm).

This is how every security-based attribute works in .NET. When the stack frame is checked in .NET, it looks at the assembly's metadata to see if any actions need to be investigated. For example, if we had a LinkDemand action on ReadFile(), *only* the immediate caller's credentials would be probed. If another application were controlling our UI application, the controlling application's credentials would be ignored. If we had used Assert, the UI code's credentials would be ignored. As you can probably surmise, using Assert makes the security checks quicker, because the stack crawl doesn't need to go as far, but it can also be a little dangerous, because the check stops at that point. If method A called method B, which made an Assert action, it wouldn't matter if A had the permission to use the resource.

Declarative vs. Imperative Security

When you use security-based attributes, the runtime will use that information to determine if a resource is accessible. This is known as *declarative security*, because you state your resource usage intentions in metadata for the world to see.[5] There is another way to control resource usage: by using imperative security. You make an explicit method call to the security action you want to invoke, and the runtime will determine if it's okay to continue. Here's what a Deny() call looks like when we change our implementation of ReadFile() to use imperative security:[6]

```
//[FileIOPermission(SecurityAction.Deny, Read=@"C:\Windows\System32")]
public int ReadFile(string filePath)
{
    int retVal = 0;

    FileIOPermission filePermDeny = new FileIOPermission(
        FileIOPermissionAccess.Read,
        Environment.SystemDirectory);
    filePermDeny.Deny();
    //  Same implementation as before...
}
```

You'll get the same results with this code as you would with the metadata attached to the method. However, the nice thing about using imperative security in this case is that we can use Environment.SystemDirectory, rather than resorting

---

5. Unfortunately, "seeing" this information isn't as easy as it sounds. We'll explain this point in more detail in the "Security and Metadata" section later in this chapter.
6. This is what the FileStream's constructor does when it verifies if a caller has access to a resource.

to hard-coding C:\Windows\System32 in a declarative attribute (which may not work on every Windows machine). Imperative security has an advantage when you cannot hard-code the resource information, or if your code has some complex Boolean logic where the security action should be applied to only a specific resource in a special case.

Security and Metadata

One advantage of declarative attributes (and attributes in general) is that they can be read via a standard API. Well, at least you would *think* that would be possible. In theory, you should be able to write a tool to read the security-based aspects of an assembly to determine what kind of security context it needs to run successfully,[7] just by reading its metadata and plucking out the attributes that derive from CodeAccessSecurityAttribute. Fortunately, .NET provides a command-line tool called Permissions View, or permview, that gets security metadata in this way.

Figure 3-3 shows the results of running permview on the FileOpener assembly. As you can see, the /decl switch will show all of the security metadata on the assembly in an XML format.

Figure 3-3. Permview results

However, there are some caveats to this approach. If an assembly decides to not publish its security needs in metadata, permview becomes useless. It works

---

7. Whether you decide to give it the permissions it needs is another story...

only with security-based attributes; imperative security calls are simply ignored.[8] Therefore, an assembly may try to use a resource that is checked by the .NET runtime, even if permview comes back with nothing. Granted, code that secures a resource should be written so that it ensures the access is valid, but from a configuration standpoint, you don't know what the assembly's intentions are.

The other issue with security-based attributes is how they are stored. Recall from the discussion in the "Compiling Attributes" section in Chapter 1 that metadata is usually stored in a `.custom` directive. Unfortunately, security-based attributes don't use the same directive. Figure 3-4 shows the results of viewing `ReadFile()` in ILDasm, which illustrates where these attributes go. As you can see, the metadata is stored in a `.permissionset` directive, not a `.custom` directive.

```
FileOpener::ReadFile : int32(string)
.method public hidebysig instance int32  ReadFile(string filePath) cil managed
{
    .permissionset deny = (3C 00 50 00 65 00 72 00 6D 00 69 00 73 00 73 00     // <.P.e.r.m.i.s.s.
                           69 00 6F 00 6E 00 53 00 65 00 74 00 20 00 63 00     // i.o.n.S.e.t. .c.
                           6C 00 61 00 73 00 73 00 3D 00 22 00 53 00 79 00     // l.a.s.s.=.".S.y.
                           73 00 74 00 65 00 6D 00 2E 00 53 00 65 00 63 00     // s.t.e.m...S.e.c.
                           75 00 72 00 69 00 74 00 79 00 2E 00 50 00 65 00     // u.r.i.t.y...P.e.
                           72 00 6D 00 69 00 73 00 73 00 69 00 6F 00 6E 00     // r.m.i.s.s.i.o.n.
```

Figure 3-4. Security metadata in an Assembly.tif

This means that the standard Reflection API cannot glean security information from an assembly, because it looks at metadata only within `.custom` directives. Therefore, unless you're willing to write your own assembly file parser to get this information, you're stuck with using permview.

NOTE   *There are some third-party libraries that have been written to parse an assembly's file structure to get access to everything within an assembly from managed code. One example of this is Microsoft's FxCop tool, which has an API that you can use to get the security metadata of an assembly (you'll see the FxCop assembly in action in Chapter 5). However, this functionality should be in the .NET Framework. We hope a future version will include this in the API.*

SOURCE CODE   *The code for these examples is in Chapter3\FileOpener and Chapter3\FileOpenerClient.*

---

8.   It's not that you couldn't write a tool to look at the CIL of every method in an assembly, along with the complete call stack of those methods, to see if any imperative security calls are made. However, performing such a process will require a lot of CPU cycles.

Platform Invoke Attributes

In Chapter 2, you learned how attributes such as `ClassInterface` and `Guid` affect the behavior of the regasm tool as it generates a type library for COM interoperability. This section, however, is concerned with another type of interoperability: .NET code calling into legacy C or C++ DLLs that define function exports. Not only does this entail new attributes, but the attributes used affect the behavior of the runtime, rather than affecting the compiler or other tools.

Studying the Role of Platform Invoke

The canonical example of useful DLLs with function exports is the Windows API. This consists of thousands of function exports spread over dozens of DLLs. Thankfully, the .NET Framework does an excellent job of wrapping this complexity in easy-to-use objects, and thus it greatly diminishes the need to access these functions directly. That said, there may still be cases where you need to invoke a Windows API function.

Another scenario requiring this form of interoperability is where you have built your own DLLs or purchased third-party libraries that export functions. Instead of completely rewriting these often complex libraries in managed .NET code, you can call them directly from any managed language.

The .NET Framework addresses both of these scenarios using a technology known as *platform invoke* (sometime abbreviated to *PInvoke*). Platform invoke provides many services, but it is primarily responsible for marshaling data between managed code (.NET) and unmanaged code (COM components and API functions). Given that the .NET Framework classes must ultimately call Windows API functions, the entire .NET Framework is built on platform invoke. Therefore, Microsoft went to extreme lengths to ensure that this technology is flexible, dependable, and robust.

Using the DllImport Attribute

In most cases, you will interact with the platform invoke services using the `DllImport` attribute. With this attribute, you can define a method that maps to a function exported from a DLL. Your .NET code can then call the exported function in the same way that it calls any other .NET method. The `DllImport` attribute has many named parameters that control the interaction, but at a minimum, you must specify the location of the DLL that defines that function. The attribute also requires that the method it decorates be marked `static` and `extern`, and that the method be empty; that is, it does not have any implementation.

For example, the code in Listing 3-2 demonstrates how to access the Windows API Beep() function. This simple function sounds a tone at the specified frequency and for the specified duration. It is defined in kernel32.dll as follows:

```
BOOL Beep(DWORD dwFreq,        // sound frequency
          DWORD dwDuration     // sound duration
);
```

Armed with this information, you can apply the DllImport attributes, as shown in Listing 3-2.

Listing 3-2. A Simple DllImport Example

```
using System.Runtime.InteropServices; // For the DllImport attribute

class TesterMain
{
    [DllImport("kernel32")]
    private static extern int Beep(int frequency, int duration);

    static void Main(string[] args)
    {
        Beep(1000, 1000);
    }
}
```

As you can see in the Main() function of this example, once the external function is properly defined and attributed with DllImport, you can invoke the function the same way you invoke any other managed method.

The code in Listing 3-2 named the .NET method the same as the API function, but this is not required. You can name the method anything you like by using the DllImport attribute's EntryPoint parameter to specify the actual function name in the DLL, as shown in the following example:

```
class TesterMain
{
    [DllImport("kernel32", EntryPoint="Beep")]
    private static extern int MyBeep(int f, int l);

    static void Main(string[] args)
    {
        MyBeep(1000, 1000);
    }
}
```

As mentioned earlier, DllImport has many named parameters like EntryPoint that allow you to further refine the interaction with an unmanaged function. Table 3-3 lists these parameters and their purpose.

Table 3-3. The Named Parameters of the DllImport Attribute

DllImport Parameter	Description
CallingConvention	Indicates which convention to use when calling the function. Settings include Cdecl, StdCall, and ThisCall. The default is WinApi, which means the calling convention is determined based on the underlying platform (StdCall for most Windows platforms; Cdecl for Windows CE).
CharSet	Specifies which character set to use when marshaling strings between managed code and the unmanaged world of the DLL. The default is Ansi, meaning that platform invoke appends an *A* onto the function name and converts all string parameters to 1-byte per character ANSI strings.
EntryPoint	Specifies the name or the ordinal of the exported function in the DLL.
ExactSpelling	When true, the exact name in EntryPoint is used to find the function in the DLL. Otherwise, some CharSet settings cause the runtime to append an *A* or a *W* to the function name. The default value is false.
PreserveSig	When false, the runtime modifies the given method signature by redefining the current return value as an [out, retval] parameter and returns an HRESULT instead. The default value is true, meaning the given signature is not modified.
SetLastError	When true, the function will call SetLastError before returning, and the calling code can retrieve the error by calling Marshal.GetLastWin32Error. The default value is false.

The parameters in Table 3-3 are useful when you must account for the internal structure of the Windows API, which is bifurcated to handle two different character sets: 8-bit ANSI characters and 16-bit Unicode characters. For example, the MessageBox() function is actually exported as MessageBoxA (the *A* suffix representing ANSI) and MessageBoxW (the *W* character representing the "wide," or Unicode, character set). With judicious use of the CharSet and ExactSpelling parameters, you can manually specify which version of the API function to use: ANSI or Unicode. For example, the following code forces the use of the Unicode version of MessageBox():

```
class TesterMain
{
    [DllImport("user32", EntryPoint="MessageBoxW",
                ExactSpelling=true, CharSet=CharSet.Unicode)]
    private static extern int MyMsgBox(int hWnd, string lpText,
        string lpCaption, uint uType );

    static void Main(string[] args)
    {
        MyMsgBox(0, "Testing", "Testing", 0);
    }
}
```

Marshaling Structures

The managed .NET runtime and the unmanaged API functions are built on vastly different type systems. The former uses types defined by the CTS and strictly enforces type safety. The latter, however, uses C or C++ data types and does not strictly enforce type safety. To bridge this gap, the platform invoke service must convert data from its managed CTS representation into corresponding unmanaged types and vice versa. It does this using a process termed *marshaling*.

Platform invoke provides standard marshaling services that marshal simple types using a default conversion scheme. In Listing 3-2, for example, platform invoke automatically converts the .NET integers (System.Int32) to DWORDs as required by the Beep() function. The marshaling mechanics get more difficult, however, when trying to convert more complex types such as structures. Although a .NET structure is analogous to a C/C++ structure, there are significant differences:

- .NET does not guarantee field ordering or packing within a structure, and therefore its actual memory layout is dynamic. Unmanaged functions, however, expect structures with a specific, static memory layout.

- .NET does not support fixed-length strings or fixed-length arrays. However, these are used extensively within structures defined in the API and consumed by unmanaged functions.

Fortunately (and predictably), the .NET Framework provides several attributes that help you overcome these differences.

Applying the StructLayout Attribute

The primary attribute used to address the structure layout issue is the aptly named StructLayout attribute. You can apply this attribute to any .NET structure or class to control its physical layout, thus making it useful for interoperating with unmanaged code. To help study this attribute, Listing 3-3 defines a simple C-style structure and function export. Assume this is compiled into a standard (that is, non-COM) DLL named CustomLibrary.dll. Upcoming examples will use this code to experiment with the StructLayout attribute and study the effects of various settings.

Listing 3-3. A C-style Structure and Function Export in CustomLibrary.DLL

```
// A simple C/C++ structure
struct Employee
{
   double Wage;
   short Hours;
};

// Initializes an Employee struct with default values
extern "C" _declspec(dllexport) void InitializeEmployee(Employee* emp)
{
   emp->Wage = 15.5;
   emp->Hours = 40;
}
```

This example defines a simple Employee structure containing fields that record the wage and hours worked for a given employee. The exported function, InitializeEmployee(), accepts an Employee structure and initializes it with some default values. Notice that the function's one parameter is actually a pointer to an Employee structure, which is the C mechanism for passing parameters by reference. Therefore, the structure will need to be marshaled in both directions: from managed to unmanaged, and then back to managed.

To call the InitializeEmployee() function, you must first define a structure that is the managed equivalent to the C-style Employee structure. You then apply the StructLayout attribute to the managed structure, as shown in Listing 3-4.

Listing 3-4. Applying the StructLayout Attribute

```
// Define a managed Employee structure
[StructLayout(LayoutKind.Sequential)]
struct Employee
{
    public double Wage;
    public short Hours;
}
```

The LayoutKind.Sequential setting informs the runtime that it should pre-serve the given field order instead of reordering as it sees fit. Now you can use this managed Employee structure to define the C# external method and invoke the InitializeEmployee() function as shown here:

```
class TesterMain
{
    [DllImport(@"..\..\..\CustomLibrary\Debug\customlibrary.dll")]
    private static extern void InitializeEmployee(ref Employee emp);

    static void Main(string[] args)
    {
        Employee emp = new Employee();
        InitializeEmployee(ref emp);
        Console.WriteLine(emp.Hours);
    }
}
```

Remember that the InitializeEmployee() function accepts a pointer to an Employee structure. Although .NET provides the IntPtr type for representing pointers, in this example it is easier to use a ref parameter in the signature of the managed InitializeEmployee() method to represent the Employee pointer (Employee*).

Using the FieldOffset Attribute

The StructLayout attribute also provides the LayoutKind.Explicit setting, which gives you complete control over the layout of the managed structure. When you apply this setting, you must explicitly specify the byte offsets of each field within the structure using the FieldOffset attribute. For example, you can rede-fine the Employee structure from Listing 3-4 using the LayoutKind.Explicit setting, as follows:

```
// Define a managed Employee structure
[StructLayout(LayoutKind.Explicit)]
struct Employee
{
    [FieldOffset(0)] public double Wage;    // doubles are 64 bit
    [FieldOffset(8)] public short Hours;
}
```

The LayoutKind.Explicit setting is most useful when interacting with an unmanaged structure containing a union. C/C++ unions allow a structure to overlay a single field with several possible data types. Unfortunately, unions are not supported directly in managed code. You can, however, interact with unions by creating a distinct field in the managed structure for each field in the union. Then use the FieldOffset attribute to specify the same offset for each field.

To demonstrate, assume you have three types of employees: grunts, sales employees, and managers. In each case, the Employee structure must record the wage and hours worked. For a sales employee, however, the structure must also record a commission value. In the case of a manager, the structure must store the number of stock options owned by the employee. Listing 3-5 (heavily) modifies the original Employee structure to meet these new requirements.

Listing 3-5. Defining a Union Within the Unmanaged Employee Structure

```
// This forces structures to be packed on 1-byte boundaries
#pragma pack(1)

// Simple enumeration
enum EmployeeType {GRUNT, SALES_EMPLOYEE, MANAGER};

// A simple C/C++ structure
struct Employee
{
    double Wage;
    short Hours;

    EmployeeType EmpType;    // What kind of employee are you?
    union                    // This field changes based on employee type
    {
        double Commission;   // Used for sales employees
        int    StockOptions; // Used for managers
        short  Zero;         // Used for grunts
    };
};
```

This example adds two new fields to the `Employee` structure. The `EmpType` field records the type of employee, which is represented as an enumeration. The second field is a union that changes based on the type of employee. The code also forces a 1-byte boundary structure packing mechanism using a `#pragma` directive. This emulates most structures defined in the Windows API and ensures that each structure is as compact as possible.

Listing 3-6 shows the corresponding changes to the `InitializeEmployee()` function. It now initializes the `Employee` structure based on the given employee type.

Listing 3-6. Updating InitializeEmployee() to Initialize the Union Field

```
// Initializes an employee structure with default values
extern "C" _declspec(dllexport)
void InitializeEmployee(Employee* emp, EmployeeType empType)
{
    emp->Hours = 40;
    emp->Wage = 15.5;
    emp->EmpType = empType;

    switch(empType)
    {
    case SALES_EMPLOYEE: // SalesEmployees earn commissions
        emp->Commission = 300.75;
        break;
    case MANAGER:        // Managers get stock options
        emp->StockOptions = 500;
        break;
    default:             // Grunts get squat
        emp->Zero = 0;
    }
}
```

That completes the updates to the CustomLibrary.dll. Turning back to managed code and the `FieldOffset` attribute, Listing 3-7 defines a managed structure that corresponds with the unmanaged `Employee` structure.

Listing 3-7. Using the FieldOffset Attribute to Handle a Union Within a Structure

```
// First, define the enumeration of employee types
enum EmployeeType {Grunt, SalesEmployee, Manager};
```

```
// Define a managed Employee structure
[StructLayout(LayoutKind.Explicit)]
struct Employee
{
    [FieldOffset(0)] public double Wage;
    [FieldOffset(8)] public short Hours;

    [FieldOffset(10)] public EmployeeType EmpType;

    // To handle unions, use the same field offset
    [FieldOffset(14)] public double Commission;
    [FieldOffset(14)] public int StockOptions;
    [FieldOffset(14)] public byte Zero;
}
```

In this example, look closely at the last three fields. Notice that the FieldOffset attribute specifies the same offset for each of them. As mentioned earlier, this is the standard technique for handling unions.

Listing 3-8 tests all these updates. First, it redefines the external InitializeEmployee() method to accept an EmployeeType enumeration. Then, in the Main() method, it calls the unmanaged InitializeEmployee() function twice to initialize a manager and a sales employee.

Listing 3-8. Testing the New and Improved InitializeEmployee Function

```
class TesterMain
{
    [DllImport(@"..\..\..\CustomLibrary\Debug\customlibrary.dll")]
    private static extern void InitializeEmployee(ref Employee emp,
        EmployeeType empType);

    static void Main(string[] args)
    {
        Employee emp = new Employee();

        InitializeEmployee(ref emp, EmployeeType.Manager);
        Console.WriteLine(emp.Hours);
        Console.WriteLine(emp.EmpType);
        Console.WriteLine(emp.StockOptions);
```

```
        InitializeEmployee(ref emp, EmployeeType.SalesEmployee);
        Console.WriteLine(emp.Hours);
        Console.WriteLine(emp.EmpType);
        Console.WriteLine(emp.Commission);
    }
}
```

Notice that after initializing a manager, this code retrieves and displays the StockOptions field. But after initializing a sales employee, the code retrieves and displays the Commission field.

Marshaling Strings with the MarshalAs Attribute

Although the StructLayout and FieldOffset attributes combine to solve many structure layout issues, there is still one remaining issue: fixed-length strings and arrays. These are commonly used in C/C++ programming but are not supported in .NET languages. So what do you do when you must provide a structure containing, for example, a fixed-length string? The solution is to apply the MarshalAs attribute.

The MarshalAs attribute allows you to explicitly define how a .NET parameter, field, or return value is marshaled between managed and unmanaged code. Remember that platform invoke defines and uses default marshaling behavior for most .NET data types. Therefore, the MarshalAs attribute is rarely required. In the case of fixed-length strings, however, it provides two settings that are perfect for solving the problem:

- The UnmanagedType.ByValTStr setting, which is specifically designed to describe fixed-length strings within structures

- A SizeConst parameter to set the size of the string (or array)

To demonstrate, Listing 3-9 again modifies the unmanaged Employee structure by adding two fixed-length string fields (actually arrays of characters) to store the first and last name of the employee. This example also updates the InitializeEmployee() function with code that initializes the two new fields with a default first and last name.

Listing 3-9. Adding Fixed-Length String Fields to the Unmanaged Employee Structure

```
// A C/C++ structure
struct Employee
{
    char FirstName[20];
    char LastName[30];
```

```
    // Rest is the same (see Listing 3-5) ...
};

// Initializes an employee structure with default values
extern "C" _declspec(dllexport)
void InitializeEmployee(Employee* emp, EmployeeType empType)
{
    // Initialize the string fields
    strcpy(emp->FirstName, "Homer");
    strcpy(emp->LastName, "Simpson");

    // Rest is the same (see Listing 3-6) ...
}
```

Turning to the managed code, the first step is again to define the equivalent managed Employee structure. This is shown in Listing 3-10.

Listing 3-10. Applying the MarshalAs Attribute to the Employee Structure

```
// Define a managed Employee structure
[StructLayout(LayoutKind.Explicit)]
struct Employee
{
    [MarshalAs(UnmanagedType.ByValTStr, SizeConst=20)]
    [FieldOffset(0)]  public string FirstName;

    [MarshalAs(UnmanagedType.ByValTStr, SizeConst=30)]
    [FieldOffset(20)]  public string LastName;

    [FieldOffset(50)] public double Wage;
    [FieldOffset(58)] public short Hours;

    [FieldOffset(60)] public EmployeeType EmpType;

    // For unions use the same field offset
    [FieldOffset(64)] public double Commission;
    [FieldOffset(64)] public int StockOptions;
    [FieldOffset(64)] public byte Zero;
}
```

This example applies the MarshalAs attribute to the FirstName and LastName fields. In each case, the SizeConst parameter setting matches the length of the corresponding field in the unmanaged structure. Also, notice that the FieldOffset attributes are adjusted to account for the two, relatively large, fields.

Finally, the code in Listing 3-11 tests these new string fields by calling `InitializeEmployee()` and displaying the resulting employee data.

Listing 3-11. Testing the Final Managed Employee Structure

```
static void Main(string[] args)
{
    Employee emp = new Employee();

    InitializeEmployee(ref emp, EmployeeType.Manager);
    Console.WriteLine(emp.FirstName);
    Console.WriteLine(emp.LastName);
    Console.WriteLine(emp.Hours);
    Console.WriteLine(emp.Wage);
    Console.WriteLine(emp.EmpType);
    Console.WriteLine(emp.StockOptions);
}
```

Figure 3-5 shows the output from this example.

Figure 3-5. The output from Listing 3-11

SOURCE CODE   *The code for this example is in Chapter3\PInvoke.*

Given its central role in the .NET universe, platform invoke is much too big to cover in a few pages. This section, however, has covered the fundamental services of platform invoke and how you can influence them using attributes such as `DllImport`, `StructLayout`, and `MarshalAs`. In the next section, you will learn about attributes that influence another important runtime service: serialization.

Serialization

The term *serialization* refers to the process of converting an object's state into a stream of data. This data stream can be in any format—binary, text, XML, and so on—as long as the format is known, so that it can be used to restore the object back into memory at a later time. The process of restoring the object is called *deserialization*. Alone, serialization is not particularly exciting. However, it is critical in nearly all applications. Once an object is serialized, the data stream can be stored in a file or database and deserialized whenever necessary. Or, the data stream can be sent across a process boundary or across a network to be deserialized and used by another application. In fact, the .NET remoting framework uses serialization to do exactly that, effectively allowing objects to be passed "by value" across the network.

In this section, you will learn how to use the serialization services provided by .NET. And, not surprisingly, you will see that attributes play a key role in controlling the behavior of the runtime during serialization.

Introducing .NET Serialization

Serialization is certainly not a new concept. Earlier serialization technologies include MFC's archive mechanism, COM's IPersistStream interface, and Visual Basic's PropertyBag object. The differences between .NET serialization and these earlier technologies can be summed up with one word: simplicity. To use any of the earlier technologies, you were required to write extensive serialization code. And although this isn't difficult code to write, it is tedious and error-prone. .NET, on the other hand, only requires that you apply a simple attribute, the Serializable attribute, to a class, structure, or enumeration. In essence, this gives the runtime "permission" to serialize the object when it must. The runtime does the rest.

Automatic serialization is possible thanks to the power of Reflection. Using Reflection, the .NET runtime can discover the fields defined in any class, structure, or enumeration, even if it is a user-defined type. Once it knows an object's fields and their types, the runtime has all the information it needs to serialize an object. During serialization, the runtime also includes the object's fully qualified type name and assembly information in the data stream.

A given object may have fields that reference other objects. And these objects can reference other objects and so on. An object can also derive from an object that derives from another object and so on. Both of these scenarios have historically complicated manual serialization code, but the .NET serialization mechanism handles them automatically. When the runtime serializes an object, it first creates an in-memory graph of all the related objects, including base objects. Then it serializes each object in the graph, recording not only the state of each object but also the relationship between objects. You just need to make sure that the object's class, each base class, and every referenced type is marked as serializable; otherwise, the runtime raises an exception.

Using the Serializable Attribute

To allow the runtime to serialize an object, you simply apply the `Serializable` attribute to the class. For example, the code in Listing 3-12 defines several serializable types representing customer data.

Listing 3-12. Defining Serializable Types

```
namespace CustomerLibrary
{
   [Serializable()]
   public class Customer
   {
      private string mName;
      private Address mAddress;

      [NonSerialized()] private OrderHistory mHistory;

      public Customer(string name, Address address)
      {
         mName = name;
         mAddress = address;
         mHistory = new OrderHistory();
      }
   }

   [Serializable()]
   public class PreferredCustomer : Customer
   {
      private double mDiscount;

      public PreferredCustomer(string name, Address address, double discount)
         : base(name, address)
      {
         mDiscount = discount;
      }
   }

   public class OrderHistory
   {  // tracks order history details for a customer
   }
```

```
public enum State
{
    AL, AZ, IL, MN, MI, ME, OH, WI // etc.
}

[Serializable()]
public struct Address
{
    public string Street;
    public string City;
    public State State;
    public int Zip;
}
}
```

This example contains several notable items. First, notice that the PreferredCustomer class derives from Customer and that the Customer class references an Address structure. All of these types are marked serializable so that the runtime can successfully serialize a PreferredCustomer object, including the Customer and Address data.

Occasionally, an object may maintain state that is transient, calculated from other fields, or too large to efficiently serialize. You can tell the runtime to skip this state during serialization by applying the NonSerialized attribute to the corresponding field. In Listing 3-12, a Customer object maintains a reference to an OrderHistory object. This object may get extremely large and will likely not be required in all instances of a Customer object. Therefore, it is marked with the NonSerialized attribute.

Listing 3-13 shows the CIL after the Customer class is compiled. Unlike custom attributes that use the .custom CIL directive, the Serializable and NonSerialized attributes compile to their own CIL directives, namely serializable and notserialized. This fact places these attributes in the pseudo-custom attribute category, as defined in Chapter 1. It also allows the runtime to more efficiently determine whether a given type or field should be serialized.

Listing 3-13. The Customer Class in CIL

```
.class public auto ansi serializable beforefieldinit Customer
        extends [mscorlib]System.Object
{
    .field private string mName
    .field private valuetype CustomerLibrary.Address mAddress
    .field private notserialized class CustomerLibrary.OrderHistory mHistory

    // Snip ...
} // end of class Customer
```

Understanding .NET Serialization Formatters

Although the `Serializable` and `NonSerialized` attributes tell the runtime *what* to serialize, these attributes do not define *how* the object should be serialized. In other words, they do not control the format of the resulting data stream. Instead, a formatter object is responsible for generating the data stream in a recognizable format.

The .NET Framework provides two built-in formatters: `BinaryFormatter` and `SoapFormatter`. Each implements the `IFormatter` interface, but the resulting data streams are very different. The `BinaryFormatter` class outputs data in a proprietary binary format. The resulting stream is compact, but only another .NET application will be able to easily deserialize it back into an object. The `SoapFormatter` class, on the other hand, outputs text conforming to the SOAP specification. This not only makes it easier for non-.NET applications to deserialize the stream back into an object, but it is also possible for humans to read and understand the contents of the stream.

Many scenarios can trigger the runtime to serialize an object. For example, any attempt to pass a serializable object across an application domain boundary causes the runtime to serialize the object using one of the built-in formatters. Or, you can explicitly serialize an object into a stream using a formatter. For example, Listing 3-14 demonstrates how to use `SoapFormatter` to serialize a `PreferredCustomer` object to a file.

Listing 3-14. Using SoapFormatter to Serialize an Object

```
using System;
using System.IO;
using System.Runtime.Serialization;

// Must also set reference to System.Runtime.Serialization.Formatters.dll
using System.Runtime.Serialization.Formatters.Soap;

namespace SerializationExample
{
    class SerializationMain
    {
        static void Main(string[] args)
        {
            // First, establish the preferred customer data
            Address addr;
            addr.Street = "121 Maple St.";
            addr.City = "Springfield";
            addr.State = State.IL;
            addr.Zip = 33333;
```

```
            PreferredCustomer pc;
            pc = new PreferredCustomer("Homer", addr, 0.20);

            // Open a file to hold the data
            Stream s = File.OpenWrite("customer.soap");

            // Create the Soap formatter and serialize to file
            IFormatter formatter = new SoapFormatter();
            formatter.Serialize(s, pc);

            s.Close();
        }
    }
}
```

This example uses SoapFormatter to serialize the object to a file named customer.soap. If you look closely at the output, shown in Figure 3-6, you can see how the state information from each object is represented in the SOAP output. Keep in mind that the Serialize() method accepts any Stream-derived object, including memory streams and network socket streams, so this serialization technique can be used in applications other than just saving the data to a file.

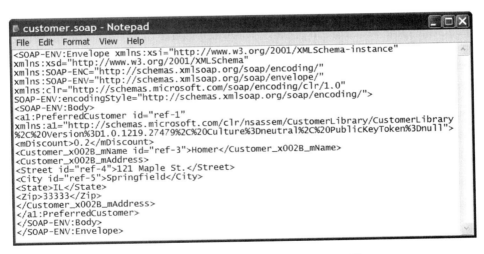

Figure 3-6. The PreferredCustomer object serialized into SOAP

You also use the formatter objects to deserialize the data back into an in-memory object. Of course, you must use the same formatter to both serialize and deserialize. Listing 3-15 demonstrates how to use the SoapFormatter.Deserialize()

method to deserialize the data in the customer.soap file into a `PreferredCustomer` object.

Listing 3-15. Deserializing the customer.soap Data

```
static PreferredCustomer DeserializeCustomer()
{
    // Open the data file for reading
    Stream s = File.OpenRead("customer.soap");

    // Create the SoapFormatter, this time for deserialization purposes
    IFormatter formatter = new SoapFormatter();

    // Deserialize, cast returned object to PreferredCustomer
    PreferredCustomer pc = (PreferredCustomer)formatter.Deserialize(s);
    s.Close();

    // Use the PreferredCustomer object ...
    return pc;
}
```

Although the `Serializable` and `NonSerialized` attributes are extremely easy to use, in some cases, you may require more control over the fields that are included in the serialization process. For example, maybe the decision to serialize a field must happen at runtime based on the value of other fields. Or, you may wish to avoid the extra cost of the reflection process the runtime uses to determine how to serialize a given object. In these situations, you need to implement the `ISerializable` interface. By implementing this interface, you can explicitly tell the runtime exactly which fields should and should not be serialized. Thus, you have much more control over the process, and the runtime does not need to perform any expensive reflection calls. Keep in mind, however, that even if you implement the `ISerializable` interface in a class, you must still decorate it with the `Serializable` attribute.

NOTE *Although implementing the* `ISerializable` *interface is a fascinating topic, it has little to do with attributes, so we won't go into any more detail here. For more information, see* Distributed .NET Programming in C# *by Tom Barnaby (Apress, 2002).*

SOURCE CODE *The code for this example is in* Chapter3\Serialization.

Using the XML Serializer

In addition to the `Serializable` attribute and the built-in formatters described in the previous sections, the .NET Framework provides another, extremely different, set of serialization classes and attributes in the `System.Xml.Serialization` namespace.

The core class in this serialization stack is the `XmlSerializer` class. This class can serialize a given object into an XML data stream and deserialize the XML stream back into an object. In many ways, this class is analogous to the `BinaryFormatter` and `SoapFormatter` classes. However, there are a few differences:

- `XmlSerializer` cannot serialize private data. It can serialize only public fields and properties.

- `XmlSerializer` requires that each class provides a default constructor.

- `XmlSerializer` does not require the `Serializable` attribute.

- `XmlSerializer` does not serialize all of the type information. Namely, it does not serialize the assembly information.

- `XmlSerializer` allows you to control the format of the XML by applying various attributes to the class or structure you wish to serialize.

Upcoming examples will demonstrate how to use the `XmlSerializer` class to serialize a `PreferredCustomer` object and its related objects as defined in Listing 3-12. To accommodate `XmlSerializer`, however, a few updates are required to these classes. Remember that `XmlSerializer` cannot serialize private data, so these customer classes must expose their serializable state using public fields or properties. Also, each class must define a default constructor, but they do not need to be marked with the `Serializable` attribute. These updates are shown in Listing 3-16.

Listing 3-16. The Customer Classes Updated for XML Serialization

```
using System.Xml.Serialization; // Must also reference System.Xml.dll
namespace CustomerLibrary
{
    // OrderHistory, State, and Address are unchanged from Listing 3-12.

    public class Customer
    {
        // Make name a private field exposed by a public property
        private string mName;
```

```csharp
      public string Name
      {
         get { return mName; }
         set { mName = value; }
      }


      // Make Home address a public field
      public Address HomeAddress;

      [XmlIgnore()]  // Tell serializer to skip the order history
      public OrderHistory mHistory;

      public Customer(string name, Address address)
      {
         mName = name;
         mAddress = address;
         mHistory = new OrderHistory();
      }

      // Default ctor required For XML Serialization
      public Customer(){}
   }

   public class PreferredCustomer : Customer
   {
      // Make discount a private field exposed by a public property
      private double mDiscount;
      public double Discount
      {
         get { return mDiscount; }
         set { mDiscount = value; }
      }

      public PreferredCustomer(string name, Address address, double discount)
         : base(name, address)
      {
         mDiscount = discount;
      }

      // Default ctor required For XML Serialization
      public PreferredCustomer() {}
   }
}
```

Beyond the previously mentioned updates, also notice that the XmlIgnore attribute adorns the Customer.mHistory field. This attribute is analogous to the NonSerialized attribute; the XmlSerializer ignores any item decorated with the XmlIgnore attribute.

Listing 3-17 shows the XmlSerializer class in action. You use it much like one of the formatters, except that you must construct the XmlSerializer object with the type information for the type you wish to serialize.

Listing 3-17. Using the XmlSerializer *Class*

```
static void Main(string[] args)
{
    // First, establish the customer data
    Address addr = new Address();
    addr.Street = "121 Maple St.";
    addr.City = "Springfield";
    addr.State = State.IL;
    addr.Zip = 33333;

    PreferredCustomer pc;
    pc = new PreferredCustomer("Homer", addr, 0.20);

    // Open a file to hold the data
    Stream s = File.OpenWrite("customer.xml");

    // Create the XmlSerializer and serialize customer to file
    XmlSerializer xs = new XmlSerializer(typeof(PreferredCustomer));
    xs.Serialize(s, pc);
    s.Close();
}
```

 NOTE *The* typeof *operator used in the previous example returns a* Type *object that holds type information for the given class. For more details, see the section titled "A Quick Reflection Review" in Chapter 4.*

The resulting customer.xml file is shown in Listing 3-18. As you can see, the output is easy to read because XmlSerializer maps the classes, fields, and properties to XML elements. Notice that the inherited members are also included in the output.

Listing 3-18. The Customer.xml File

```xml
<?xml version="1.0"?>
<PreferredCustomer xmlns:xsd="http://www.w3.org/2001/XMLSchema"
                    xmlns:xsi="http://www.w3.org/2001/XMLSchema-instance">
  <HomeAddress>
    <Street>121 Maple St.</Street>
    <City>Springfield</City>
    <State>IL</State>
    <Zip>33333</Zip>
  </HomeAddress>
  <Name>Homer</Name>
  <Discount>0.2</Discount>
</PreferredCustomer>
```

Using the XML Serialization Attributes

In addition to the XmlSerializer class, the System.Xml.Serialization namespace defines dozens of attributes that affect the behavior of the XmlSerializer. For example, you can apply attributes to a class, field, or property to change its corresponding XML element name. You can also map a field or property to an XML attribute. Listing 3-19 demonstrates several of these attributes.

Listing 3-19. Applying XML Serialization Attributes

```csharp
namespace CustomerLibrary
{
    // OrderHistory, State, and Address are unchanged from Listing 3-12

    public class Customer
    {
        private string mName;

        [XmlAttribute("Name")]  // Serialize this as an attribute
        public string Name
        {
            get { return mName; }
            set { mName = value; }
        }

        // Make Home address a public field
        public Address HomeAddress;
```

```csharp
   [XmlIgnore()]   // Tell serializer to skip the order history
   public OrderHistory mHistory;

   public Customer(string name, Address address)
   {
      mName = name;
      HomeAddress = address;
      mHistory = new OrderHistory();
   }

   // Default ctor required For XML Serialization
   public Customer(){}
}

[XmlRoot("VIP")] // Serialize as a VIP root element
public class PreferredCustomer : Customer
{
   private double mDiscount;

   // Serialize to a CustomerDiscount element
   [XmlElement("CustomerDiscount")]
   public double Discount
   {
      get { return mDiscount; }
      set { mDiscount = value; }
   }

   public PreferredCustomer(string name, Address address, double discount)
      : base(name, address)
   {
      mDiscount = discount;
   }
   // Default ctor required For XML Serialization
   public PreferredCustomer() {}
   }
}
```

This example uses the XmlAttribute, XmlRoot, and XmlElement attributes to change the way XmlSerializer serializes the object. Listing 3-20 shows the output when a PreferredCustomer object is serialized.

Listing 3-20. The Effect of the XML Serialization Attributes

```xml
<?xml version="1.0"?>
<VIP xmlns:xsd="http://www.w3.org/2001/XMLSchema"
     xmlns:xsi="http://www.w3.org/2001/XMLSchema-instance"
    Name="Homer">
  <HomeAddress>
    <Street>121 Maple St.</Street>
    <City>Springfield</City>
    <State>IL</State>
    <Zip>33333</Zip>
  </HomeAddress>
  <CustomerDiscount>0.2</CustomerDiscount>
</VIP>
```

The System.Xml.Serialization namespace also defines the XmlArray attribute, which you can use to control the serialization of an array of objects. For example, Listing 3-21 finally fills in the details of the OrderHistory class used in the previous examples. Notice that it contains an array of Order objects.

Listing 3-21. Using the XmlArray Attribute

```csharp
namespace CustomerLibrary
{
    public class Order
    {
        [XmlAttribute()]
        public int Id;
        public double Total;
        public DateTime Date;
    }

    public class OrderHistory
    {
        [XmlArray(), XmlArrayItem("OrderItem")]
        public Order[] Orders;

        public double ComputeTotal()
        {
            double total = 0;
            if (Orders != null)
```

```
        {
            foreach(Order order in Orders)
                total += order.Total;
        }
        return total;
    }
  }
}
```

In addition to the XmlArray attribute, this example also applies the XmlArrayItem attribute. This optional attribute allows you to specify the XML element name used for each individual item in the array. For example, if you were to serialize an OrderHistory object, the output would look like Listing 3-22.

Listing 3-22. A Serialized OrderHistory Object

```xml
<?xml version="1.0"?>
<OrderHistory xmlns:xsd="http://www.w3.org/2001/XMLSchema"
              xmlns:xsi="http://www.w3.org/2001/XMLSchema-instance">
  <Orders>
    <OrderItem Id="1">
      <Total>100</Total>
      <Date>2003-05-11T00:00:00.0000000-05:00</Date>
    </OrderItem>
    <OrderItem Id="2">
      <Total>200</Total>
      <Date>2003-05-11T00:00:00.0000000-05:00</Date>
    </OrderItem>
    <OrderItem Id="3">
      <Total>300</Total>
      <Date>2003-05-11T00:00:00.0000000-05:00</Date>
    </OrderItem>
  </Orders>
</OrderHistory>
```

Table 3-4 summarizes the attributes that control the XML serialization process. In addition to these attributes, the System.Xml.Serialization namespace defines SOAP-related attributes that force XmlSerializer to output data conforming to the SOAP specification. Most of these SOAP-related attributes mirror those available for XML serialization.

Table 3-4. The XML Serialization Attributes

Attribute	Applies To	Description
XmlAnyAttribute, XmlAnyElement	Any public field, property, parameter, or return value that returns an array of XmlAttribute objects	Used during deserialization to handle data unknown to the schema.
XmlArray, XmlArrayItem	Any field, property, parameter, or return value that returns an array of complex objects	Controls the serialization of members that represent arrays of custom types.
XmlAttribute	Public field, property, parameter, or return value	Marks a member that should be serialized as an XML attribute
XmlChoiceIdentifier	Public field, property, parameter, or return value	Associates a string member with a range of valid choices contained in an enumeration or array of strings
XmlElement	Public field, property, parameter, or return value	Marks a member that should be serialized as an XML element
XmlEnum	Public field, property, parameter, or return value	Controls how an enumeration member is serialized
XmlIgnore	Public field or property	Marks a member that should not be serialized
XmlInclude	Public derived class or return value	Useful in Web services; includes the specified type in the generated WSDL document
XmlRoot	Public class	Defines the root element of the XML document
XmlText	Public field or property	Marks a member that should be serialized as XML text
XmlType	Public class	Controls how the XML schema is generated during serialization

As you can see, the overall list of attributes related to XML serialization is extensive. And although this section has not thoroughly investigated each one, it has covered the essential attributes and how they are applied. Armed with this, you should be able to research the details of the remaining attributes and easily apply them as well.

SOURCE CODE *The code for this example is in Chapter3\XMLSerialization.*

Remoting and Context

Most modern operating systems, including the various flavors of Windows, isolate a running application within the confines of a process. A process is an application boundary that acts like a fortress, protecting a running application from interference from other running applications. However, sometimes you may wish to share information with or use the services of another application executing within a separate process. Although operating systems provide various inter-process communication (IPC) mechanisms, these are typically low-level services and are difficult to use. Therefore, .NET provides a number of services that abstract most (but not all) of the complexities involved with IPC. Collectively, these services are grouped into a technology called *remoting*.

This section reviews the basics of remoting while focusing on the related attributes. It will also cover how .NET uses a concept known as *context*, which will be important in understanding the upcoming discussions regarding enterprise services and building custom attributes.

Remoting Attributes

Although the operating system executes an application within a process, the .NET runtime provides another application boundary called an *application domain*. Like a process, an application domain provides an isolation boundary around your application to ensure that its resources cannot be directly accessed by other applications. Unlike a process, however, multiple application domains can exist within a single process.

When you create an object, you allocate and initialize memory owned by the current application domain. Therefore, a typical object is application domain bound; that is, it must execute within the application domain where it was created. If you wish to expose the object to other application domains, you have two choices:

- Expose the object as a *marshal-by-reference object*. In this case, the object remains inside the original application domain, but other application domains can reference it and invoke its methods.

- Expose the object as a *marshal-by-value object*. In this case, the object can be copied from the original application domain to another application domain, which can then use the copied object in the same way as any other local object.

The following sections detail these two choices and their related attributes.

Marshal-by-Reference and the OneWay Attribute

To create a marshal-by-reference object, you must derive the object's class from MarshalByRefObject, as shown in Listing 3-23. This code defines a simple CustomerService class and compiles it into a CustomerLibrary.dll assembly.

Listing 3-23. Defining a Marshal-by-Reference Object (CustomerLibrary.dll)

```
namespace CustomerLibrary
{
    public class CustomerService : MarshalByRefObject
    {
        public double GetTotalExpenditures(int customerId)
        {
            // Query database and calculate the total sum the
            // customer has spent on our products.
            return 1400; // A simulated value
        }
    }
}
```

Once you have defined the remote object, you must build a .NET application to host the object and expose it to remote clients. To accomplish this, you use various services found in the System.Runtime.Remoting namespace to programmatically register the class with the .NET remoting framework. This framework manages most of the details of exposing the object to client applications and handles incoming requests from them. Listing 3-24 demonstrates how to expose the CustomerService object using the remoting framework.

Listing 3-24. Exposing a Marshal-by-Reference Object (CustomerServer.exe)

```
using System.Runtime.Remoting;
using System.Runtime.Remoting.Channels;
using System.Runtime.Remoting.Channels.Http;

class ServerMain
{
    static void Main(string[] args)
    {
        // Establish channel and open port 13101
        IChannel channel = new HttpChannel(13101);
        ChannelServices.RegisterChannel(channel);
```

```
    // Configure CustomerServices as a well-known singleton object
    RemotingConfiguration.RegisterWellKnownServiceType(
        typeof(CustomerLibrary.CustomerService),
        "CustomerService.soap",
        WellKnownObjectMode.Singleton);

    // Keep running until user presses enter
    Console.WriteLine("Server started. Press enter to end.");
    Console.ReadLine();
    }
}
```

Now that the object is exposed by the CustomerServer application, client
applications can connect to the remote CustomerService object and call its methods. Just like the hosting application, a .NET client application uses services in
the .NET remoting framework to establish a connection to the remote object.
This is demonstrated in Listing 3-25.

Listing 3-25. A Client Connecting to a Remote Object

```
using System.Runtime.Remoting;
using CustomerLibrary;

class ClientMain
{
    static void Main(string[] args)
    {
        // Create a local proxy to the remote object.
        object remote = Activator.GetObject(typeof(CustomerService),
            "http://localhost:13101/CustomerService.soap");

        CustomerService custSvc = (CustomerService)remote;

        Console.WriteLine(custSvc.GetTotalExpenditures(1));
    }
}
```

In this example, the Activator.GetObject() method creates and returns
a client-side proxy object. This proxy object exposes the same interface (that is,
public methods, properties, and events) as the remote object. In other words, it
impersonates the remote object. When the client invokes a method on the proxy,
it passes the method call to the remoting framework plumbing that consists of

channels, message sinks, and formatters (the same formatters used to serialize objects). These framework objects team up to serialize the method call into a message and send it across the network to the server application domain (that is, the application domain hosting the remote object). The server application domain's remoting framework deserializes the incoming request using the same channel, message sinks, and formatter and invokes the method on the remoted object. Any return values or exceptions are then sent through the same plumbing back to the client.

> **NOTE** *.NET remoting is an enormous topic. For more details on .NET remoting, see* Distributed .NET Programming in C# *by Tom Barnaby (Apress, 2002). For an even more advanced treatment, see* Advanced .NET Remoting (C# Edition) *by Ingo Rammer (Apress, 2002).*

The point is that a method call on a remote object can take a long time. And while the method call is making its way through the remoting plumbing, the client thread that made the call is blocked, waiting for the return values. In other words, the remote method call is *synchronous*. In some cases, however, the method may not return any values, or remote clients may not care about the returned values or possible exceptions. Therefore, there is no reason for the client thread to block while waiting for the remote method to complete. In these cases, you want to allow the client to invoke the method and continue on; you want an *asynchronous* method call.

The .NET Framework provides a number of mechanisms to allow asynchronous remote method calls, but the easiest by far is to apply the OneWay attribute. When you apply this attribute to a method on a remotable object, there are two side effects:

- For calls originating from remote clients, the runtime does not bother to establish the remote plumbing for any return values, which greatly reduces the overhead of the remote call.

- From the client's point of view, the method call executes asynchronously.

Listing 3-26 demonstrates the use of the OneWay attribute.

Listing 3-26. Applying the OneWay Attribute

```
namespace CustomerLibrary
{
    using System.Runtime.Remoting.Messaging; // Contains OneWay attr
    using System.Threading;
```

```
public class CustomerService : MarshalByRefObject
{
    public double GetTotalExpenditures(int customerId)
    {
        // Query database and calculate the total sum the
        // customer has spent on our products.
        return 1400; // A simulated value
    }

    [OneWay()]
    public void Save(int id, string name, string email)
    {
        // Save customer data to database

        // Sleep for 5 seconds to simulate long running task
        Thread.Sleep(5000);
    }
}
}
```

This example adds a Save() method to the CustomerService class. Because the method does not define any ref or out parameters, and because it does not return a value, it is a good candidate for the OneWay attribute. Listing 3-27 implements a client that invokes the Save() method.

Listing 3-27. Invoking a OneWay Method

```
class ClientMain
{
    static void Main(string[] args)
    {
        // Create a local proxy to the remote object.
        object remote = Activator.GetObject(typeof(CustomerService),
            "http://localhost:13101/CustomerService.soap");

        CustomerService custSvc = (CustomerService)remote;

        Console.WriteLine("Begin Save method ...");
        custSvc.Save(1, "Homer", "hs@atomic.com");
        Console.WriteLine("End Save method");
    }
}
```

If you try this code for yourself, compare the behavior of the client application with and without the OneWay attribute applied to the Save() method. Without the attribute, the client application halts for approximately five seconds on the call to Save(). With the OneWay attribute, the Save() method returns immediately, allowing the client to continue executing.

Marshal-by-Value and the Serializable Attribute

In addition to marshal-by-reference objects, .NET remoting also supports marshal-by-value objects. While marshal-by-reference objects are accessed via a client side proxy, marshal-by-value objects are copied from the remote application domain into the client's application domain. Therefore, all client access occurs entirely on a client-side object.

Recall that a key component of the remoting plumbing is a formatter that serializes method calls into messages that can be sent across the network. It so happens that this formatter can be either BinaryFormatter or SoapFormatter, which were discussed earlier in this chapter, in the "Understanding .NET Serialization Formatters" section. Therefore, the remoting framework can serialize any object marked with the Serializable attribute and pass it as part of the message. The receiving application domain can then deserialize the object from the message and use it in the same way as it uses any other local object.

For example, Listing 3-28 defines a simple Customer class. The primary purpose of this class is to collect information regarding a given customer. So, rather than forcing clients to interact with the object remotely, you can mark it as serializable and let the runtime copy it from the server application to the requesting client.

Listing 3-28. A Simple Serializable Customer Class

```
[Serializable()]
public class Customer
{
    private int mId;
    private string mName;
    private string mEmail;

    public Customer(int id, string name, string email)
    {
        mId = id;
        mName = name;
        mEmail = email;
    }
```

```
   public int Id
   {
      get { return mId; }
      set { mId = value; }
   }
   public string Name
   {
      get { return mName; }
      set { mName = value; }
   }
   public string Email
   {
      get { return mEmail; }
      set { mEmail = value; }
   }
}
```

To test this marshal-by-value behavior, Listing 3-29 shows an updated CustomerService class sporting a new GetCustomer() method. Notice that the method returns a Customer object that is copied by-value back to the client.

Listing 3-29. The CustomerService.GetCustomer() Method

```
public class CustomerService : MarshalByRefObject
{
   public Customer GetCustomer(int customerId)
   {
      // Look up customer in database and return.
      return new Customer(1, "Homer Simpson", "hs@atomic.com");
   }

   // The rest is the same as Listing 3-26 ...
}
```

For the final test, Listing 3-30 shows the updated client application that calls the GetCustomer() method.

Listing 3-30. Retrieving the Marshal-by-Value Customer Object

```
class ClientMain
{
   static void Main(string[] args)
   {
```

```
        // Create a local proxy to the remote object.
        object remote = Activator.GetObject(typeof(CustomerService),
            "http://localhost:13101/CustomerService.soap");

        // Cast the proxy to the CustomerService type
        CustomerService custSvc = (CustomerService)remote;

        // Fetch a customer
        Customer cust = custSvc.GetCustomer(1);

        // Call a property on the local object
        Console.WriteLine(cust.Name);

        // ...
    }
}
```

SOURCE CODE   *The code for this example is in Chapter3\Remoting.*

Context Attributes

Like an application domain, a context is a type of boundary. A single application domain can contain many contexts, but it must have a least one called the *default context*. Contexts provide the following services:

- An environment consisting of a set of properties shared by all objects in the context

- An interception boundary, so that the runtime can provide preprocessing and postprocessing on all method calls originating from outside the context

- A home for objects with similar runtime requirements such as synchronization, thread affinity, or just-in-time (JIT) activation

Most .NET objects are *context agile*, meaning that the runtime creates them within the default context and they can freely move from one context to another. When you acquire a reference to a context agile object, it is a direct reference. Therefore, it is impossible to intercept method calls made on a context agile object.

On the other hand, if a class derives from ContextBoundObject, then instances are *context bound*. When the runtime creates a context-bound object, it investigates the object's context requirements and places it within a compatible context where it must remain for its entire lifetime. If a compatible context does not exist, the runtime creates one. Any client code executing outside this context never holds a direct reference to the context-bound object. Instead, a reference to a context-bound object is actually a reference to a runtime-generated proxy. Like the proxy created in a remoting scenario, this proxy converts every method call made on the reference into a message object and passes this message into the context containing the actual object. While crossing the context boundary, the runtime can intercept the message and apply any required preprocessing. It can also intercept the method's return value and provide any required postprocessing. This mechanism allows the runtime to provide a number of services.

Applying the Synchronization Attribute

One runtime service that relies on context is synchronization. You can request this service using the Synchronization attribute (from the System.Runtime.Remoting.Contexts namespace). When you apply this attribute to a class derived from ContextBoundObject, the runtime ensures that only one thread at a time can access the object. This makes the entire object safe for multithreading. It accomplishes this by creating the object within a context and intercepting any incoming method calls. Listing 3-31 demonstrates how to use the Synchronization attribute.

Listing 3-31. Using the Synchronization Context Attribute

```
// Required for Synchronization attribute
using System.Runtime.Remoting.Contexts;

[Synchronization()]
public class NumberDispenser : ContextBoundObject
{
    private int mCurrentNumber;

    public int TakeANumber()
    {
        mCurrentNumber++;
        return mCurrentNumber;
    }
}
```

This simple NumberDispenser class simulates the take-a-number devices located at customer service desks everywhere. Its task is easy—to increment and return a number—but if two threads called the TakeANumber() method at the

same time, they could each get the same number. However, thanks to the
Synchronization attribute, this cannot happen. For example, a calling thread
could invoke the TakeANumber() method like this:

```
static void Main(string[] args)
{
    NumberDispenser nd = new NumberDispenser();
    int i = nd.TakeANumber();
}
```

When this happens, the .NET runtime will intercept the call. If another thread is
already executing within the NumberDispenser object, it will force this method call
to wait until the thread exits the object. Figure 3.7 shows how this works.

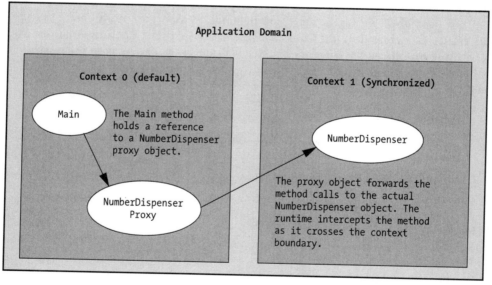

Figure 3-7. The .NET context interception mechanism

This context interception mechanism is highly extensible. In Chapter 4, you
will see how to include your own context interception logic using custom context attributes. And in the next section, you will see how .NET uses the context
concept to provide enterprise services such as automatic transactions and
object pooling.

SOURCE CODE   *The code for this example is in Chapter3\Context.*

Applying the ContextStatic and ThreadStatic Attributes

Most likely, if you have written classes in C#, Visual Basic .NET, or C++, you have defined several class fields as static (or Shared in Visual Basic .NET). When a field is marked static, its value is shared across all instances of the class. This is true for all instances, regardless of the context in which they are currently executing. However, the .NET runtime also supplies a ContextStatic attribute that you can apply to any static field if you wish it to be shared only by those objects executing in the same context.

For example, Listing 3-32 defines a CountMe class with a standard static field and a context static field. Note that the class is also synchronized, and therefore the runtime must create it within its own synchronized context.

Listing 3-32. Applying the ContextStatic Attribute

```
[Synchronization()]
class CountMe : ContextBoundObject
{
    private static int mStaticCount = 0;

    [ContextStatic()]
    private static int mContextCount = 0;

    public CountMe()
    {
        mStaticCount++;
        mContextCount++;
    }

    public int StaticCount
    {
        get { return mStaticCount; }
    }

    public int ContextCount
    {
        get { return mContextCount; }
    }

    public int GetContextId()
    {
        return Thread.CurrentContext.ContextID;
    }
}
```

As you can see, the constructor of the `CountMe` class increments both the static count and the context static count. Notice that both the `StaticCount` and `ContextCount` properties are instance properties. Static methods always run within the caller's context, so making these properties nonstatic ensures that the code executes within the `CountMe` object's context.

To test the `ContextStatic` functionality, the code in Listing 3-33 creates two `CountMe` objects and displays their respective context IDs. It then displays the static count and the context static count for one of the `CountMe` objects.

Listing 3-33. Testing the ContextStatic Attribute

```
class ContextStaticMain
{
    static void Main(string[] args)
    {
        CountMe c1 = new CountMe();
        CountMe c2 = new CountMe();

        Console.WriteLine("Context ID for c1 = {0}", c1.GetContextId());
        Console.WriteLine("Context ID for c2 = {0}", c2.GetContextId());
        Console.WriteLine("Static count = {0}", c1.StaticCount);
        Console.WriteLine("Context count = {0}", c1.ContextCount);
    }
}
```

The output, shown in Figure 3-8, proves that the objects are running in separate contexts and that each context has its own context static count.

Figure 3-8. The output from Listing 3-33

Somewhat related to the `ContextStatic` attribute is the `ThreadStatic` attribute. Like the `ContextStatic` attribute, the `ThreadStatic` attribute can be applied to any static field. However, a thread static field's value is shared across all objects executing in the current thread.

SOURCE CODE   *The code for this example is in Chapter3\ContextStatic.*

Enterprise Services Attributes

In the late 1990s, Microsoft observed that many developers were writing large amounts of infrastructure code to provide complex services such as thread pooling, object pooling, distributed transactions, and security. Although these services are necessary for enterprise applications, they are not trivial to implement and have little to do with the core business problem. Microsoft recognized the need for a generic solution to these problems and developed a technology called Microsoft Transaction Server (MTS). Since then, the technology has undergone several updates and name changes. For example, the Windows 2000 operating system included an updated version of MTS called COM+. And now, with the advent of .NET, the services provided by COM+ are collectively known as *enterprise services*, even though COM+ itself remains relatively unchanged.

This section will demonstrate how .NET attributes and contexts work together to allow COM+ to host .NET objects and provide enterprise services to these objects.

Investigating the COM+ Context

In the previous section, you learned how the .NET context concept allows the runtime to provide services such as object synchronization. This context concept, however, is not new. In fact, it originated with COM+.

The COM+ context serves the same purpose as the .NET context. However, there are a couple differences:

- COM+ contexts are configured using the Component Services administration tool. .NET contexts are configured using special context attributes applied to items in the code.

- The COM+ context requirements for a given object are stored in a machine-wide database called the *COM+ catalog*. .NET context requirements are stored within the assembly in the form of attribute metadata.

Surveying the Enterprise Service Attributes

Despite the differences between the COM+ and .NET contexts, when you build a .NET object that requires COM+ services (enterprise services), you use the familiar mechanisms of attributes and .NET contexts. The System.EnterpriseServices namespace defines several .NET attributes that mirror the settings available through the Component Services administration tool. Therefore, instead of using a tool to configure the object, in .NET you simply apply the appropriate attribute. The enterprise service attributes are summarized in Table 3-5.

Table 3-5. Enterprise Service Attributes

COM+ Service	.NET Attribute	Description
Application activation	ApplicationActivation	Apply to assembly. Specifies where the serviced object runs: in the creator's process or within the COM+ service process (Dllhost.exe).
Application name	ApplicationName	Apply to assembly. Specifies the name of the COM+ application as it appears in the Component Services administration tool.
Auto completion	AutoComplete	Apply to serviced class method. If the method returns without exception, the runtime destroys the object and does not doom the transaction. If the method raises an exception, the runtime destroys the object and dooms the transaction.
Automatic transactions	Transaction	Apply to serviced class. Specifies the level of transaction support required by the object.
Construction string	ConstructionEnabled	Apply to serviced class. When the serviced object is activated, the given string is passed into the object for initializing object state. The string can be updated by developers or administrators.
Event tracking	EventTrackingEnabled	Apply to serviced class. Allows COM+ to gather usage statistics and display them in the Component Services tool.
Just-in-time activation	JustInTimeActivation	Apply to serviced class. COM+ only activates the object when a client invokes a method. Typically, the object is then immediately deactivated.
Object pooling	ObjectPooling	Apply to serviced class. COM+ will allocate a pool of objects. When activating the object, COM+ simply grabs it from the pool. When deactivating, COM+ puts it back in the pool.
Queued interface	InterfaceQueuing	Apply to a serviced class. Specifies an implemented interface that should be process as a queued interface. The specified interface must not define any by-reference parameters or return values.

Table 3-5. Enterprise Service Attributes (continued)

COM+ Service	.NET Attribute	Description
Queued exception	ExceptionClass	Apply to serviced class. Specifies the object to create if a queued component errors while processing a message. The message is "played back" on the exception object.
Role based security	SecurityRole	Apply to assembly, serviced class, interface, or method. Configures a COM+ security role and allows members of the role to access the attributed item.
Synchronization	Synchronization	Apply to serviced class. Tells COM+ to provide synchronized access to the object, thus ensuring only one thread can access it at a time.

Like the other .NET attributes, the enterprise service-related attributes are compiled into the assembly metadata. Unfortunately, the COM+ runtime knows nothing about assembly metadata. Remember that the COM+ runtime reads the COM+ catalog to determine if the object has special context requirements. Therefore, after the assembly is compiled, the COM+ configuration information stored in the metadata must be copied into the COM+ catalog.

Fortunately, the .NET Framework comes with a tool that does exactly that. The .NET Services Installation tool (regsvcs.exe) reads the metadata from a given assembly and copies any COM+-related information into the COM+ catalog. At this point, the .NET object appears to COM+ like any other COM+ component. You can even see the .NET assembly and any serviced object listed in the Component Services administration tool.

Applying an Enterprise Service Attribute

Now, let's walk through the creation of a .NET class that requires the COM+ JIT activation service. Listing 3-34 demonstrates the general pattern for using an enterprise services attribute. Assume this class is defined within a CustomerLibrary.dll assembly.

Listing 3-34. Using the JustInTimeActivation Attribute

```
[JustInTimeActivation()]
public class CustomerService : ServicedComponent
{
    // Default ctor is required
    public CustomerService() {}

    // Implementation ...
}
```

This example applies the JustInTimeActivation attribute to a class, advertising that each CustomerService object requires JIT activation services from COM+. Also, note that the CustomerService class derives from ServicedComponent class. This is required by most enterprise attributes. The ServicedComponent base class serves a number of purposes:

- Tools such as regsvcs look for this base class to determine which classes need to be registered with COM+.

- The class provides default implementations for two common COM+ interfaces: IObjectControl and IObjectConstruct.

- ServicedComponent derives from ContextBoundObject. Therefore, all classes deriving from ServicedComponent are also context-bound objects. When an object derives from ServicedComponent, it is referred to as a *serviced object*.

To help prove that the object is activated within a COM+ context, Listing 3-35 adds a GetContextInfo() method that returns a string displaying some information about the COM+ context. The code uses the ContextUtil class to gather the COM+ context information.

Listing 3-35. The CustomerService.GetContextInfo() Method

```
[JustInTimeActivation()]
public class CustomerService : ServicedComponent
{
    public CustomerService() {}

    public string GetContextInfo()
    {
        StringBuilder ctxInfo = new StringBuilder();
```

```
    // Use ContextUtil to fetch context information
    ctxInfo.AppendFormat("Context ID:  {0}\n", ContextUtil.ContextId);
    ctxInfo.AppendFormat("Activity ID: {0}\n", ContextUtil.ActivityId);

    // If in transaction, get transaction ID
    string txId = "No Tx";
    if (ContextUtil.IsInTransaction)
        txId = ContextUtil.TransactionId.ToString();

    ctxInfo.AppendFormat("Transaction ID:    {0}\n", txId);
    ctxInfo.AppendFormat("Security Enabled?: {0}\n",
        ContextUtil.IsSecurityEnabled);

    return ctxInfo.ToString();
  }
}
```

Compiling and Registering the Serviced Class

Assemblies containing serviced classes must be strong-named if you wish them to be hosted by the COM+ runtime. Therefore, as described Chapter 2, you must apply the `AssemblyKeyFile` attribute to the assembly. Typically, this is done in the AssemblyInfo.cs file, as shown in Listing 3-36. This listing also demonstrates the use of a couple other attributes: `ApplicationName` and `ApplicationActivation`.

Listing 3-36. The AssemblyInfo.cs File

```
// Set strong name and version
[assembly: AssemblyKeyFile(@"d:\MyKey.snk")]
[assembly: AssemblyVersion("1.0.0.0")]

// Change the name of the application as it appears in the COM+ tool
[assembly: ApplicationName("My Customer Library")]

// Set the application activation style to library
[assembly: ApplicationActivation(ActivationOption.Library)]
```

After compiling the CustomerLibrary.dll assembly, the next step is to execute regsvcs. This copies all of the enterprise services metadata to the COM+ catalog.

```
regsvcs CustomerLibrary.dll
```

Figure 3-9 shows the effect this has within the Component Services administration tool. Notice that it now shows a My Customer Library application with a `CustomerService` component node underneath.

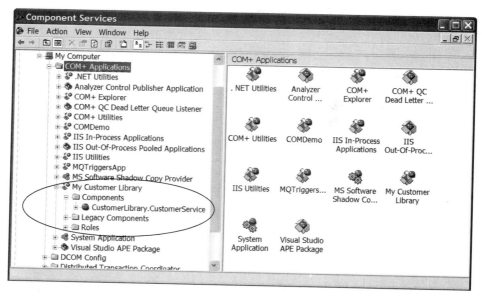

Figure 3-9. The My Customer Library application in the administration tool

Finally, Listing 3-37 shows a simple client to test the CustomerService class. Notice that this code simply creates the `CustomerService` object and uses it normally. However, through the magic of context and interception, the object is actually created within the COM+ context.

Listing 3-37. A Client for CustomerService

```csharp
using System;
using System.EnterpriseServices; // must also set reference
using CustomerLibrary;

namespace CustomerClient
{
    class ClientMain
    {
        static void Main(string[] args)
        {
            CustomerService cs = new CustomerService();
            Console.WriteLine(cs.GetContextInfo());
        }
    }
}
```

The output, shown in Figure 3-10, proves that the object was created within the COM+ context.

```
D:\Apress\Attributes\c3\Scratch\EnterpriseServices\CustomerClient\bin\Debug\Custo...
Context ID:  cc485271-cf31-4a96-b341-26b80c85359c
Activity ID: 1b42283c-b698-40a8-bca0-00a989e2d012
Transaction ID:   No Tx
Security Enabled?: False

Press any key to continue_
```

Figure 3-10. Output generated from Listing 3-37

Obviously, COM+ and its various enterprise services is a vast topic. The goal in this section was to demonstrate how context and attributes make .NET integration with COM+ possible and to give you an idea of how it works. For additional information and details on .NET and COM+, see *Distributed .NET Programming in C#* by Tom Barnaby (Apress, 2002).

SOURCE CODE   *The code for this example is in Chapter3\EnterpriseServices.*

Conclusion

In this chapter, you learned the following:

- How to use declarative security

- How to interact with platform invoke services

- How to use various attributes to control the .NET serialization services (including XML serialization)

- How to apply the OneWay attribute for asynchronous remote method calls

- How .NET uses context and context attributes to provide services such as synchronization

- How context attributes allow COM+ to host .NET objects and provide enterprise services

Throughout this chapter and previous chapters, you have seen a variety of ways that attributes affect day-to-day development in .NET. Because attributes are so prevalent, coverage of these attributes quickly becomes an overview of .NET itself; not only have you learned about a variety of attributes, but you have also learned how key services such as security, interoperability, and serialization work in .NET.

The following chapters study attributes under a different light. Instead of looking at predefined attributes, they focus on how you can create your own custom attributes and apply them as effectively as Microsoft has throughout the .NET Framework. The next chapter begins this process by discussing the basics of developing custom attributes. Chapter 5 builds on these ideas by leading you through a real-world application of custom attributes.

CHAPTER 4

Building Custom Attributes

SO FAR, WE HAVE FOCUSED on attributes defined and used by either the compiler or the .NET runtime. As an example, consider the `Serializable` attribute. Given that the runtime defines this attribute, it is perfectly reasonable that the runtime can look for its application in code and respond appropriately. The preceding chapters have shown how .NET applies attributes throughout the .NET Framework to provide important functionality such as COM interoperability, serialization, security, and integration with COM+ services. Clearly, Microsoft developers felt that attributes were a useful construct and used them heavily when designing the framework.

I have always maintained that anything good enough for the largest software company in the world is good enough for me. Therefore, this chapter shows how you and I, or any .NET developer, can also take advantage of attributes by defining and using *custom attributes*. After describing the mechanics of defining and applying a custom attribute, the chapter discusses how you can use Reflection to discover and respond to custom attributes. To demonstrate the utility of custom attributes, the chapter builds a simple custom attribute that decorates classes with developer contact information. Finally, the chapter covers context attributes and shows how you can use the context-interception mechanism to implement a new development philosophy called Aspect Oriented Programming (AOP). All of these techniques will be used again in Chapter 5, which leads you through another realistic, and complex, application of custom attributes.

Defining Custom Attributes

Two questions normally arise when discussing custom attributes:

- How do I create a custom attribute?

- Why should I care?

This section focuses on the first question by examining the syntax and runtime support for creating custom attributes. The second question, which is more important and more difficult to answer, is addressed in later sections.

Creating a Simple Custom Attribute

To define a custom attribute, you simply create a class that derives from the System.Attribute class. By convention, you should always add an Attribute suffix to the class name. The following example demonstrates creating a custom attribute class:

```
sealed class MyCustomAttribute : System.Attribute
{ }
```

Just like built-in attributes, custom attributes do not need the Attribute suffix when you apply them, as in this example:

```
[MyCustom]
class SomeClass
{ }
```

As Figure 4-1 shows, when this class is compiled, the resulting CIL code includes a .custom tag that specifies the MyCustomAttribute class. Again, this is exactly how the compiler handles built-in attributes.

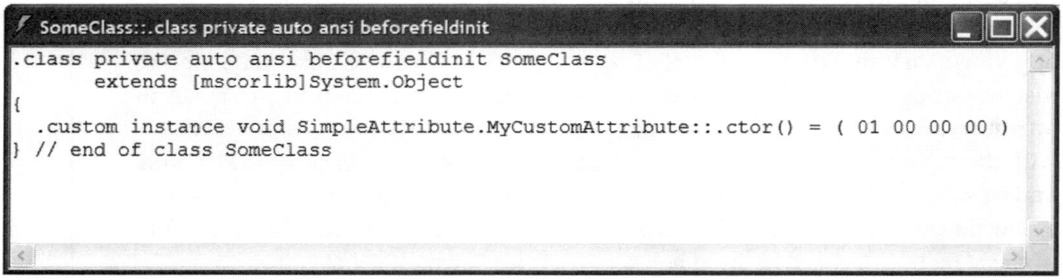

```
SomeClass::.class private auto ansi beforefieldinit
.class private auto ansi beforefieldinit SomeClass
       extends [mscorlib]System.Object
{
  .custom instance void SimpleAttribute.MyCustomAttribute::.ctor() = ( 01 00 00 00 )
} // end of class SomeClass
```

Figure 4-1. MyCustomAttribute in CIL

Restricting Attribute Usage

Currently, the sample custom attribute can decorate any code item: classes, structures, interfaces, methods, and so on. However, you typically design attributes to adorn specific code items, such as classes and structures only or methods only. Likewise, most built-in attributes are also restricted in which code items they can decorate. For example, you can apply the SynchronizationAttribute only to a class.

To specify exactly which code items your custom attribute should decorate, you can apply the AttributeUsageAttribute to the custom attribute class, as shown in the following example:

```
[AttributeUsage(AttributeTargets.Class)]
sealed class MyCustomAttribute : System.Attribute
{ }
```

The `AttributeUsageAttribute` constructor accepts an `AttributeTargets` enumeration. This enumeration lists all the code items that can possibly be decorated with attributes. The following code shows the definition of the `AttributeTargets` enumeration:

```
[Flags(), Serializable()]
enum AttributeTargets
{
    Assembly, Module, Class, Enum, Struct, Constructor,
    Method, Property, Field, Event, Interface, Parameter,
    Delegate, ReturnType,

    // The All enumerator is a union of every target type.
    All = Assembly | Module | Class | Enum | Struct |
          Constructor | Method | Property | Field | Event |
          Interface | Parameter | Delegate | ReturnType
}
```

As you can see, the `AttributeTargets` enumeration is decorated with the `Flags` attribute. When this attribute is applied to an enumeration, the runtime automatically sets the values of each element so that they can be combined together with a bitwise OR operator. Notice that the `AttributeTargets.All` element ORs all the other elements together to create a union of every possible attribute target. The `AttributeTargets.All` element is also the default setting, so if you do not apply the `AttributesUsage` attribute, the custom attribute can be applied to any code item.

TIP *By convention, all enumerations adorned with the* `Flags` *attribute are named in the plural form; for example,* `AttributeTargets`.

Currently, the `MyCustom` attribute can be applied only to classes. However, the following application of the `AttributeUsage` attribute specifies that the custom attribute can be applied to classes, structures, and interfaces:

```
[AttributeUsage(AttributeTargets.Class | AttributeTargets.Interface
      | AttributeTargets.Struct)]
sealed class MyCustomAttribute : System.Attribute
{ }

[MyCustom]
class SomeClass
{ }

[MyCustom]
struct SomeStructure
{}

[MyCustom]
interface ISomeInterface
{}
```

Defining Positional and Named Parameters

A custom attribute is a class, and like any class, it can have any number of constructors and properties defined within it. In the case of custom attributes, however, these familiar constructs take on a slightly different meaning and nomenclature. Namely, constructors morph into *positional parameters* and properties are known as *named parameters*. When you apply an attribute, you are required to provide all positional parameters in their correct order. However, named parameters are optional, and you can apply them in any order you wish. Let's look at an example to see how this works.

To begin, let's create a more useful custom attribute named DeveloperInfoAttribute. The purpose of this attribute is to document the contact information for the developer responsible for a code item. Let's assume we have two absolutely necessary bits of developer information we need to record: the developer's name and e-mail address. On the other hand, a work phone number and mobile phone number are useful, but not required. The custom attribute shown in Listing 4-1 addresses these requirements.

Listing 4-1. The DeveloperInfoAttribute Custom Attribute

```
[AttributeUsage(AttributeTargets.Class | AttributeTargets.Struct
      | AttributeTargets.Interface)]
sealed class DeveloperInfoAttribute : Attribute
{
    private string mName;
    private string mEmail;
    private string mWorkPhone = string.Empty;
    private string mMobilePhone = string.Empty;
```

```
public DeveloperInfoAttribute(string name, string email)
{
    mName = name;
    mEmail = email;
}

public string Name
{
    get { return mName; }
}
public string Email
{
    get { return mEmail; }
}
public string WorkPhone
{
    get { return mWorkPhone; }
    set { mWorkPhone = value; }
}
public string MobilePhone
{
    get { return mMobilePhone; }
    set { mMobilePhone = value; }
}
}
```

Obviously, you could use this class like any other class by calling the constructor and setting the various properties. Here is an example:

```
DeveloperInfoAttribute devInfo;
devInfo = new DeveloperInfoAttribute("Homer Simpson", "hs@atomic.com");
devInfo.WorkPhone = "555-5555";
devInfo.MobilePhone = "777-7777";
```

But that is not how attributes are typically used. Instead, the attribute is intended for use on code items such as the following class:

```
[DeveloperInfo("Homer Simpson", "hs@atomic.com")]
class SomeClass
{}
```

As this example shows, you can use the attribute's constructor to provide the developer name and e-mail information while applying the attribute to a code item. In fact, because it is the only constructor defined, you must provide these parameters to avoid a compiler error. And as with any other constructor call, you must pass the parameters in the correct order, hence the term *positional parameters*.

Now what about the work and mobile phone numbers? For these attribute properties, .NET languages provide a special syntax that allows you to set the properties as needed when applying the attribute. The C# syntax is shown in the following example:

```
[DeveloperInfo("Homer Simpson", "hs@atomic.com", WorkPhone="555-5555",
    MobilePhone="777-7777")]
class SomeClass
{}
```

The syntax, as you can see, is straightforward. Simply name the property and assign it within the "constructor" call; hence these are termed *named properties*. You can also assign named properties in any order, with the following restrictions:

- Named properties must appear after all positional properties.

- Named properties can appear only once.

Applying AttributeUsage *Named Parameters*

The AttributeUsage attribute also defines three named parameters in addition to the AttributeTargets positional parameter. Table 4-1 describes these named parameters.

Table 4-1. AttributeUsage *Named Parameters*

Parameter	Type	Description
AllowMultiple	boolean	Indicates whether the attribute can be applied multiple times to the same code item. The default is false.
Inherited	boolean	Indicates whether code items deriving from or overriding the attribute target should inherit the attribute. The default is true.

The following example demonstrates the effect of the AllowMultiple parameter. You will see examples of the Inherited property later in this chapter.

```
[AttributeUsage(AttributeTargets.Class, AllowMultiple=true)]
sealed class DeveloperInfoAttribute : Attribute
{ // ...
}

// This compiles only if the AttributeUsage.AllowMultiple parameter
// is set to true.
[DeveloperInfo("Homer Simpson", "hs@atomic.com"),
 DeveloperInfo("Marge Simpson", "ms@atomic.com")]
class SomeClass
{}
```

Applying Custom Attributes

The previous section focused on the mechanics of defining and applying custom attributes. In this section, we will tackle the more important question of how you can actually use custom attributes in your applications.

The utility of built-in attributes is fairly obvious. When you apply a built-in attribute, the compiler or runtime detects it and responds accordingly. However, neither the runtime nor the compiler know anything about a custom attribute that you define. They cannot test for the existence of it and alter their behavior. So what is the point? It turns out that custom attributes are useful only to the extent that a client uses Reflection to discover the custom attribute, read its values, and take the appropriate action. The exact response to the attribute is completely dependent on the client code, or more accurately, the developer writing the client code.

A Quick Reflection Review

Recall that assemblies use metadata to fully describe themselves, down to each class, each method, and each private field declared within them. The process of retrieving this type information at runtime is called *Reflection*. With Reflection, you can discover all the types defined within an assembly. Given any one of those types, you can list all of the properties, fields, and methods it defines. But most important, at least as far as this chapter is concerned, Reflection also allows you to retrieve all of the custom attributes applied to any of these code items.

The key class in Reflection is System.Type. This is your window into the metadata for a specific type defined in the assembly. It is an abstract class, so you will never directly create an instance with the new keyword. Instead, C# provides a typeof operator that constructs the appropriate Type object given a type name. You can also grab a Type object by calling an object's GetType() method (inherited from

System.Object), or you can invoke the static GetType() method on the Type class itself. The following code demonstrates all of these techniques.

```
// The many ways of getting a Type object ...
Type t;

// Use the typeof operator
t = typeof(SomeClass);

// Use the GetType method inherited from Object
t = new SomeClass().GetType();

// Use the static Type.GetType method.
// String format: "<namespace>.<classname>, <assemblyname>"
t = Type.GetType("SomeNamespace.SomeClass, SomeAssembly");
```

Once you have a Type object, you can use it to invoke the GetMethods() method, which retrieves an array of MethodInfo objects. Each MethodInfo object contains metadata for a method in the class. For example, the following code demonstrates how to reflect over the methods of a type.

```
t = typeof(SomeClass);
foreach (MethodInfo mi in t.GetMethods())
{
    Console.WriteLine(mi.ToString());
}
```

You have likely already guessed that the Type class also implements methods such as GetProperties(), GetFields(), GetConstructors(), and so on, which return arrays of PropertyInfo, FieldInfo, and ConstructorInfo objects, respectively. More to the point, the Type class also implements a GetCustomAttributes() method that retrieves an array of all the custom attributes applied to the type. However, this is only one of several techniques to retrieve custom attributes, as you will learn in the next section.

Discovering Custom Attributes with Reflection

Recall from Chapter 1 that the key functionality of attributes is their ability to extend the assembly metadata with custom information. When an attribute is compiled, it is stored in the assembly as a blob of metadata attached to the item it decorates in code. And like other assembly metadata, you can discover and read this information using Reflection.

Consider the following example, which applies the DeveloperInfo attribute to a class:

```
[DeveloperInfo("Homer Simpson", "hs@atomic.com", WorkPhone="555-5555",
   MobilePhone="777-7777")]
class SomeClass
{}
```

When this code is compiled, the following CIL is generated. Notice how the attribute's parameter values are serialized and stored in the assembly as metadata.

```
.class private auto ansi beforefieldinit SomeClass
        extends [mscorlib]System.Object
{
  .custom instance void DeveloperAttribute.DeveloperInfoAttribute::.ctor(
    string, string)
    = ( 01 00 0D 48 6F 6D 65 72 20 53 69 6D 70 73 6F 6E   // ...Homer Simpson
        0D 68 73 40 61 74 6F 6D 69 63 2E 63 6F 6D 02 00   // .hs@atomic.com..
        54 0E 09 57 6F 72 6B 50 68 6F 6E 65 07 35 35 35   // T..WorkPhone.555
        2D 35 35 35 54 0E 0B 4D 6F 62 69 6C 65 50 68 6F   // -555T..MobilePho
        6E 65 08 37 37 37 2D 37 37 37 37 )                // ne.777-7777

  // Rest of class CIL cut ...
}
```

 NOTE   *See the Appendix for details on the serialization format used by the runtime to generate the blob of metadata you see in the previous example.*

The .NET Reflection service provides a number of ways to retrieve this attribute information. One technique is to use the static `Attribute.GetCustomAttribute()` method, as shown in Listing 4-2.

Listing 4-2. Retrieving Custom Attributes with GetCustomAttribute

```
static void Main(string[] args)
{
    DeveloperInfoAttribute devInfo;

    // Retrieve the DeveloperInfo attribute
    devInfo = (DeveloperInfoAttribute)Attribute.GetCustomAttribute(
        typeof(SomeClass),               // Type to search
        typeof(DeveloperInfoAttribute)); // Attribute to retrieve
```

```
    // Display the developer info
    Console.WriteLine("Developer Name={0};Email={1};Work={2};Mobile={3}",
        devInfo.Name, devInfo.Email, devInfo.WorkPhone, devInfo.MobilePhone);
}
```

This example calls the method while passing two Type objects. The first Type object specifies the type to be searched, and the second specifies the requested attribute. If the requested attribute is found, the runtime creates an instance of the attribute type by deserializing the blob stored in the assembly. The method returns null if the requested attribute is not found. The output from Listing 4-2 is shown in Figure 4-2.

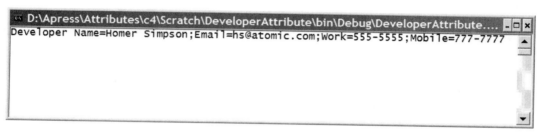

Figure 4-2. Listing 4-2 output

The GetCustomAttribute() method is overloaded several times to enable the retrieval of attributes attached to any code item. One such overload accepts a MemberInfo object as the first parameter. This allows you to retrieve custom attributes applied to methods, properties, events, and fields. For example, assume that the DeveloperInfo attribute can be applied to methods, as shown here:

```
[DeveloperInfo("Homer Simpson", "hs@atomic.com", WorkPhone="555-5555",
    MobilePhone="777-7777")]
class SomeClass
{
    [DeveloperInfo("Marge Simpson", "ms@atomic.com", WorkPhone="555-555",
        MobilePhone="777-7777")]
    public void SomeMethod()
    {}
}
```

Given the previous SomeClass definition, the following code retrieves the DeveloperInfo attribute from SomeMethod():

```
static void Main(string[] args)
{
    DeveloperInfoAttribute devInfo;
```

```
// Get member information for SomeMethod
MemberInfo mi = typeof(SomeClass).GetMethod("SomeMethod");

// Retrieve attribute on SomeMethod
devInfo = (DeveloperInfoAttribute)Attribute.GetCustomAttribute(
    mi, typeof(DeveloperInfoAttribute));
}
```

Similarly, the `Attribute.GetCustomAttribute()` method is overloaded several times to allow you to retrieve a specified attribute on an assembly, module, or parameter.

The `Attribute` class also defines a `GetCustomAttributes()` method that returns an array of all attributes or all attributes of a given type applied to a given code item. You can then easily loop through the array and search for a specific attribute or take action on each of the attributes. For example, consider the `SomeClass` definition shown in Listing 4-3.

Listing 4-3. SomeClass with Many Applied Attributes

```
[DeveloperInfo("Homer Simpson", "hs@atomic.com")]
[DeveloperInfo("Marge Simpson", "ms@atomic.com")]
[Serializable]
[Obsolete("Might as well use VB6 buddy")]
public class SomeClass
{   // ...
}
```

As you can see, this class now has four attributes applied, including two `DeveloperInfo` attributes. In this case, if you try to use the `GetCustomAttribute()` method to retrieve the `DeveloperInfo` attribute, it raises an exception, as in this example:

```
// Causes an exception because there are multiple DeveloperInfo attrs!
devInfo = (DeveloperInfoAttribute)Attribute.GetCustomAttribute(
    typeof(SomeClass),
    typeof(DeveloperInfoAttribute));
```

However, you can call `GetCustomAttributes()` instead to retrieve all of the applied `DeveloperInfo` attributes, like this:

```
// Retrieve all the applied DeveloperInfo attributes
Attribute[] attributes = Attribute.GetCustomAttributes(typeof(SomeClass),
    typeof(DeveloperInfoAttribute));
```

When retrieving attributes by a given attribute type, these Reflection methods match and return instances of both the exact attribute type and attributes derived from the given attribute. To help minimize the searching and Reflection required, it is recommended that you seal each of your custom attribute classes, unless you plan on the attribute class being used as a base class for another custom attribute. A sealed attribute eliminates the need for the attribute Reflection methods to continue searching for other derived attributes and therefore improves performance.

You can also use the GetCustomAttributes() method to retrieve all of the attributes applied to a code item, regardless of attribute type, by simply excluding the second parameter. The example in Listing 4-4 uses this method to retrieve all the attributes applied to SomeClass and displays the full type name of each attribute.

Listing 4-4. Retrieving All of the Custom Attributes on SomeClass

```
static void Main(string[] args)
{

    // Retrieve all the applied DeveloperInfo attributes
    Attribute[] attributes = Attribute.GetCustomAttributes(typeof(SomeClass));

    foreach(Attribute attr in attributes)
    {
        // Display the attribute type
        Console.WriteLine(attr.GetType());
    }
}
```

The output from Listing 4-4 is shown in Figure 4-3.

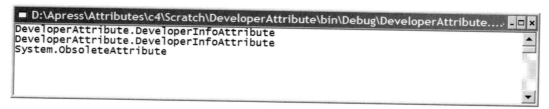

Figure 4-3. Listing 4-4 output

Comparing the output in Figure 4-3 to the actual attributes applied to the class in Listing 4-3, you will see that one attribute—the Serializable attribute—is missing. This is because the Serializable attribute is not technically a custom attribute; it is a pseudo-custom attribute. Recall from Chapter 1 that a pseudo-custom attribute does not extend the type metadata; instead, it simply sets the value of predefined metadata.

The GetCustomAttribute() family of methods does not extract pseudo-custom attributes. However, this information is usually available through other means. For example, the Type.Attributes property returns a TypeAttributes enumeration that you can use to query for a variety of pseudo-custom attributes and other class characteristics, such as its visibility, whether it is sealed, and so on. Listing 4-5 extends the previous example by using the Type.Attributes property to display other noncustom attributes.

Listing 4-5. Retrieving the Pseudo-Custom Attributes

```
static void Main(string[] args)
{
    // Retrieve all the applied DeveloperInfo attributes
    Attribute[] attributes = Attribute.GetCustomAttributes(typeof(SomeClass));

    foreach(Attribute attr in attributes)
    {
        // Display the attribute type
        Console.WriteLine(attr.GetType());
    }

    Type t = typeof(SomeClass);

    // Is SomeClass serializable?
    bool isSerializable = (TypeAttributes.Serializable & t.Attributes) != 0;
    Console.WriteLine("Serializable? {0}", isSerializable);

    // Show all the pseudo-custom attributes on SomeClass
    Console.WriteLine("Other attributes: {0}", t.Attributes);
}
```

The output from this example is shown in Figure 4-4.

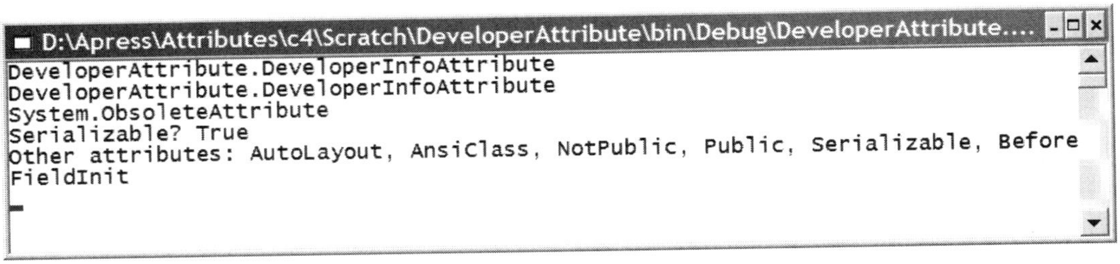

Figure 4-4. Listing 4-5 output

The previous section on Reflection highlighted the fact that you can use the Type class to retrieve information regarding the methods, properties, events, and fields that are defined within a given type. As you might expect, the Type class also allows you to retrieve all the attributes applied to a particular type. The following example shows how to get the SomeClass attributes:

```
static void Main(string[] args)
{
    // Use the Type class to retrieve all of the attributes on SomeClass
    Type t = typeof(SomeClass);
    object[] attributes = t.GetCustomAttributes(false);

    foreach(object attr in attributes)
    {
        // Display the attribute type
        Console.WriteLine(attr.GetType());
    }
}
```

This example invokes the Type.GetCustomAttributes() method and passes a boolean value indicating whether to consider inherited attributes; that is, attributes applied to base classes of SomeClass (see the next section for further details on this parameter). Another item to note is that the Type.GetCustomAttributes() method returns an array of generic object instances instead of an array of Attribute instances.

An overload of the Type.GetCustomAttributes() method allows you to retrieve only a specified custom attribute. For example, the following code retrieves all the DeveloperInfo attributes applied to SomeClass:

```
static void Main(string[] args)
{
    // Use the Type class to retrieve only the DeveloperInfo attrs
    Type t = typeof(SomeClass);
    object[] attributes = t.GetCustomAttributes(
        typeof(DeveloperInfoAttribute), false);

    foreach(object attr in attributes)
    {
        // Display the attribute type
        Console.WriteLine(attr.GetType().FullName);
    }
}
```

Interestingly, the Type class inherits this GetCustomAttributes() functionality from the MemberInfo class. Other classes deriving from MemberInfo include

MethodInfo, PropertyInfo, EventInfo, and more. Therefore, you can also use these classes to retrieve the attributes applied to their respective code items. In addition, the runtime defines an interface named ICustomAttributeProvider, which specifies the GetCustomAttributes() behavior implemented by the MemberInfo class and several other classes.

So far, this section has covered many techniques for retrieving attributes. However, it is impossible to cover all the combinations of different code items and different method overloads. Fortunately, they all follow the patterns established in the provided examples. Table 4-2 summarizes the runtime classes that support custom attribute retrieval.

Table 4-2. Runtime Classes That Support Custom Attribute Retrieval

Class	Notes
Assembly	Implements the ICustomAttributeProvider interface to retrieve custom attributes applied to the current assembly. Ignores the inherit parameter of the GetCustomAttributes() method.
Attribute	Provides two static methods for custom attribute retrieval: GetCustomAttribute() and GetCustomAttributes(). Each is overloaded many times to support retrieval for any of the code items that accept attributes.
MemberInfo	Implements the ICustomAttributeProvider interface and is a base class for MethodInfo, PropertyInfo, EventInfo, FieldInfo, ConstructorInfo, and Type. Each of these classes overrides the GetCustomAttributes() method to retrieve the attributes on its respective code item.
Module	Implements the ICustomAttributeProvider interface to retrieve custom attributes applied to the current module. Ignores the inherit parameter of the GetCustomAttributes() method.
ParameterInfo	Implements the ICustomAttributeProvider interface to retrieve custom attributes applied to the current parameter. Ignores the inherit parameter of the GetCustomAttributes() method.

Inheritance and Custom Attributes

As you have seen in the previous section, the methods for retrieving custom attributes include a provision for finding inherited custom attributes. Remember that when you're defining a custom attribute, you have the option of allowing it to be inherited by items derived from the original attribute target. You can specify this by setting the AttributeUsageAttribute.Inherited named parameter when applying the AttributeUsage attribute, as shown in the following example:

```
[AttributeUsage(AttributeTargets.All, AllowMultiple=true, Inherited=true)]
sealed class DeveloperInfoAttribute : Attribute
{
    public override string ToString()
    {
        return string.Format("Name={0}", mName);
    }
    // Snipped the rest ...
}
```

This example also shows an added ToString() override in the DeveloperInfoAttribute class. This will be used in upcoming examples to distinguish between different attribute instances.

We will also use the types defined in Listing 4-6 to experiment with retrieving inherited custom attributes. Notice that this code sets the DeveloperInfoAttribute.Name property of each attribute to easily identify its location in the class structure.

Listing 4-6. Class Structure for Inherited Attributes Examples

```
[DeveloperInfo("Base Class Attr", "hs@atomic.com")]
[Serializable]
[Obsolete("Might as well use VB6 buddy")]
public class BaseClass
{
    [DeveloperInfo("BaseClass.SomeMethod attr", "ms@atomic.com")]
    public virtual void SomeMethod()
    {}
}

[DeveloperInfo("Derived Class Attr", "hs@atomic.com")]
public class DerivedClass : BaseClass
{
    [DeveloperInfo("DerivedClass.SomeMethod attr", "ms@atomic.com")]
    public override void SomeMethod()
    {}
}
```

Listing 4-7 shows how to retrieve all the attributes, including inherited attributes, on the DerivedClass using the Attribute.GetCustomAttributes() method.

Listing 4-7. Displaying All Attributes with Attribute.GetCustomAttributes()

```
static void Main(string[] args)
{
    // Retrieve all the applied DeveloperInfo attributes
    Attribute[] attributes = Attribute.GetCustomAttributes(typeof(DerivedClass));

    foreach(Attribute attr in attributes)
    {
        // Display the attribute name and type
        Console.WriteLine("{0}, {1}", attr, attr.GetType());
    }
    Console.ReadLine();
}
```

In the output shown in Figure 4-5, notice that the inherited attribute is shown along with the attribute applied directly to the DerivedClass. This is the default behavior of the static Attribute.GetCustomAttributes() method. Also notice that the DerivedClass class does not inherit either the Serializable attribute or the Obsolete attribute.

Figure 4-5. Listing 4-7 output

Certain overloads of Attribute.GetCustomAttributes() accept a boolean parameter indicating whether to consider inherited attributes. To ignore inherited attributes, you must explicitly set this parameter to false, as shown in the following example:

```
Attribute[] attributes = Attribute.GetCustomAttributes(
    typeof(DerivedClass), false);
```

In addition, the ICustomAttributeInterface.GetCustomAttributes() method (implemented by MemberInfo among many other classes) requires you to provide this parameter. Therefore, the code in Listing 4-8 also produces the same output as shown in Figure 4-5.

Listing 4-8. Displaying All Attributes with Type.GetCustomAttributes()

```
static void Main(string[] args)
{
   // Retrieve all the applied DeveloperInfo attributes
   Type t = typeof(DerivedClass);
   object[] attributes = t.GetCustomAttributes(true);

   foreach(object attr in attributes)
   {
      // Display the attribute type
      Console.WriteLine("{0}, {1}", attr, attr.GetType().FullName);
   }
   Console.ReadLine();
}
```

A class member can also inherit custom attributes from the base class member it overrides. For example, in Listing 4-6, notice that BaseClass defines a SomeMethod() method that is overridden in the DerivedClass. Listing 4-9 demonstrates how to retrieve the attributes applied to both BaseClass.SomeMethod() and DerivedClass.SomeMethod().

Listing 4-9. Retrieving Inherited Custom Attributes

```
static void Main(string[] args)
{
   // Get the attributes applied to DerivedClass.SomeMethod including
   // those inherited from BaseClass.SomeMethod.
   Type t = typeof(DerivedClass);
   MethodInfo mi = t.GetMethod("SomeMethod");
   object[] attributes = mi.GetCustomAttributes(
      typeof(DeveloperInfoAttribute), true);

   foreach(object attr in attributes)
   {
      // Display the attribute info
      Console.WriteLine("{0}, {1}", attr, attr.GetType());
   }
   Console.ReadLine();
}
```

Figure 4-6 shows the output of this example.

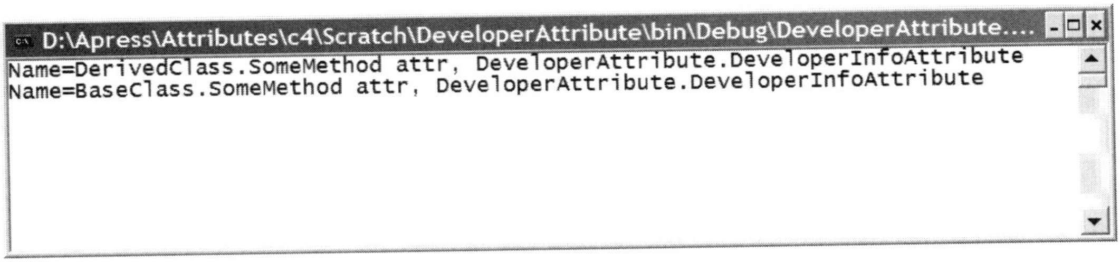

Figure 4-6. Listing 4-9 output

One other `AttributeUsage` setting also affects attribute inheritance behavior: the `AttributeUsage.AllowMultiple` property. Normally, this property specifies whether you can apply multiple instances of the same attribute to a single code item. However, a code item can also inherit a duplicate attribute. In this case, if you want to retrieve the inherited attributes, the attribute must have `AllowMultiple` set to `true`. Otherwise, you can retrieve only the attributes applied directly to the code item.

Using the DeveloperInfo Attribute

The previous sections explained the mechanics behind creating a custom attribute and how to discover the custom attribute at runtime. This section finally addresses the question of why you would want to use a custom attribute by demonstrating the utility of the `DeveloperInfo` attribute.

In isolation, the `DeveloperInfo` attribute is fairly useless; the information simply sits in the assembly as metadata. However, when the client code specifically retrieves the attribute via Reflection, it can use it to add the developer information to exceptions raised by the attributed code item. A client catching the exception can then display the developer information along with the rest of the exception details. In this way, the attribute can help a system tester track down the responsible developer when an exception occurs during testing.

The first step is to create a custom exception class. This class will handle the `DeveloperInfo` attribute retrieval and provide the information to any client code catching the exception. Listing 4-10 demonstrates how to create the custom exception class.

Listing 4-10. The CustomException Class

```
public class CustomException : ApplicationException
{
    private DeveloperInfoAttribute mDevInfo;
```

```
      public CustomException(Exception e, object sourceObject)
         : base(e.Message, e)
      {
         // Retrieve the DeveloperInfo attribute applied to the given
         // source object.
         mDevInfo = (DeveloperInfoAttribute)Attribute.GetCustomAttribute(
            sourceObject.GetType(), typeof(DeveloperInfoAttribute), false);
      }


      public DeveloperInfoAttribute DeveloperInfo
      {
         get {return mDevInfo;}
      }


      public override string ToString()
      {
         return string.Format("{0}\nDeveloper Information:{1}",
            base.ToString(), mDevInfo.ToString());
      }
   }
}
```

A CustomException object is constructed with a given Exception object and
a source object. The constructor uses the given Exception object to construct the
base ApplicationException object. Then the constructor retrieves the DeveloperInfo
attribute from the given source object and stores the reference in a field exposed
via a read-only property. The CustomException class also overrides the ToString()
method to include the developer information within the returned string. Notice
that the implementation actually relies on the DeveloperInfoAttribute.ToString()
method to do the majority of the work. This means that this method should be
beefed up from its earlier implementation. These changes are shown here:

```
public class DeveloperInfoAttribute : Attribute
{
   public override string ToString()
   {
      return string.Format("Name={0};Email={1};Work Phone={2};Mobile Phone={3}",
         mName, mEmail, mWorkPhone, mMobilePhone);
   }
   // the rest is the same ...
}
```

Now application code can raise a CustomException object instead of the generic
ApplicationException object. For example, the Demo class shown in Listing 4-11
catches a forced divide-by-zero exception and raises a CustomException instead.

Listing 4-11. Raising the CustomException

```
[DeveloperInfo("Homer", "hs@atomic.com", WorkPhone="555-5555")]
public class Demo
{
    public void DemoMethod()
    {
        try
        {
            ForceException();
        }
        catch(Exception e)
        {
            CustomException custom = new CustomException(e, this);
            throw custom;
        }
    }

    private void ForceException()
    {
        int zero = 0;
        int i = 5 / zero;
    }
}
```

In this example, notice that the Demo class is decorated with the DeveloperInfoAttribute. Also notice the forced DivideByZeroException is caught and passed into the constructor along with a reference to the current (Demo) object. This allows the CustomException constructor to retrieve the DeveloperInfo attribute applied to the Demo object. Finally, the code raises the CustomException up the call stack.

Of course, it is ultimately the responsibility of the user interface portion of the application to catch the CustomException and handle it cleanly, possibly by displaying a message box or logging the error. But, for the sake of demonstration, the following example lets the exception pass beyond the Main() method.

```
static void Main(string[] args)
{
    Demo demo = new Demo();
    demo.DemoMethod();   // Exception raised here
}
```

In the resulting output, shown in Figure 4-7, notice that the developer information appears at the end of the exception dump.

```
D:\Apress\Attributes\c4\Scratch\DeveloperAttribute\bin\Debug\DeveloperAttribute...

Unhandled Exception: DeveloperAttribute.CustomException: Attempted to divide by
zero. ---> System.DivideByZeroException: Attempted to divide by zero.
   at DeveloperAttribute.Demo.ForceException() in d:\apress\attributes\c4\scratc
h\developerattribute\demo.cs:line 24
   at DeveloperAttribute.Demo.DemoMethod() in d:\apress\attributes\c4\scratch\de
veloperattribute\demo.cs:line 12
   --- End of inner exception stack trace ---
   at DeveloperAttribute.Demo.DemoMethod() in d:\apress\attributes\c4\scratch\de
veloperattribute\demo.cs:line 17
   at DeveloperAttribute.TheApp.Main(String[] args) in d:\apress\attributes\c4\s
cratch\developerattribute\main.cs:line 12
Developer Information:Name=Homer;Email=hs@atomic.com;Work Phone=555-5555;Mobile
Phone=
Press any key to continue
```

Figure 4-7. Output showing the CustomException

SOURCE CODE   *The complete code for the* DeveloperInfo *attribute example is in Chapter4\DeveloperInfoAttribute.*

Developing Context Attributes

As useful as the DeveloperInfo attribute currently is, it requires that developers follow a couple of conventions:

- Each class should be decorated with the DeveloperInfo attribute.

- Each class should capture any system exception and raise a CustomException object in its place.

Although you cannot avoid the first convention, you can, with a little extra work, avoid the second.

To remove the need for the second convention, you can leverage the context architecture discussed in Chapter 3. Remember that the context provides an interception boundary whereby the runtime can apply preprocessing and postprocessing on each method call originating from outside the context. The runtime uses interception to provide many different services such as synchronization, automatic transactions, and security. Thanks to the highly extensible nature of the .NET runtime, you can insert your own interception logic using a special type of attribute, called a *context attribute*. However, the interaction between custom attributes, context, the runtime, and various other supporting classes and interfaces is fairly complex. So before developing a useful context attribute, you first need a thorough understanding of context and the interception mechanisms it employs.

CAUTION *Much of what follows is undocumented runtime func-tionality. It is likely that many of the context-interception mechanisms discussed here will be rewritten in the next major release of the .NET Framework. However, the major concepts— context, interceptions, message, message sinks, and so on—are sure to remain, even if some of the implementation details change.*

Rethinking Method Calls

Most developers intuitively understand method calls. To fully understand the discussion that follows, however, you may need to rethink some of the assumptions you make when you call a method.

The mechanics of a typical method call consist of copying the parameter data to the stack, jumping to the memory address where the method code lives, and then reading the parameters off the stack and executing the method. This process is complicated by virtual and abstract methods, but the core details remain the same.

Early object-oriented pioneers had a different view of method calls. They saw a method call as a message passed from one object to another. At a high level of abstraction, this view is accurate if you think of the method parameters as the contents of the message and the stack as the medium that transfers the message.

This message-oriented view of method calls helps to explain what happens when you invoke a method on a context-bound object. Recall from Chapter 3 that every .NET application runs within an application domain, which, in turn, can contain many contexts. Also recall that if a class derives from `ContextBoundObject`, instances of the class must be activated within a given context and remain there for life. Furthermore, client code executing outside this context never holds a direct reference to the context-bound object. Instead, a reference to a context-bound object actually refers to a runtime-generated proxy. This proxy converts every method call made on the reference into a message object and passes it to the context containing the actual object.

The .NET Framework defines several classes that represent a method call as a message. Most of these classes are intended for only internal use and are poorly documented. However, the framework also defines several documented interfaces that the message classes may implement. For example, all message classes implement the `IMessage` interface. Table 4-3 lists all of the message-related interfaces.

Table 4-3. The Message-Related Interfaces

Message Interface	Inherits	Description
IMessage	NA	The base interface that all message interfaces inherit
IMethodMessage	IMessage	Represents all messages that are method calls and method returns
IMethodCallMessage	IMethodMessage, IMessage	Represents a method call message
IMethodReturnMessage	IMethodMessage, IMessage	Represents a method return message
IConstructionCallMessage	IMethodCallMessage, IMethodMessage, IMessage	Represents a constructor call message
IConstructionReturnMessage	IMethodReturnMessage, IMethodMessage, IMessage	Represents a constructor return message

The primary purpose of each interface listed in Table 4-3 is to provide a way to investigate the details of the method call while it is in message form. What is the name of the method? What parameters are provided? What are the values of these parameters? Using the message-related interfaces, you can answer these and other questions about the method call. Listing 4-12 demonstrates how to retrieve this information from a given message object.

Listing 4-12. Experimenting with the IMethodCallMessage Interface

```
private void MessageDemo(IMessage msg)
{
    // Cast IMessage param to IMethodCallMessage
    IMethodCallMessage methodCall = null;
    if((methodCall = msg as IMethodCallMessage) != null)
    {
        // Display the name of the method
        Console.WriteLine("Method Name: {0}", methodCall.MethodName);

        // Display the type that is receiving the method
        Console.WriteLine("Method call target: {0}", methodCall.TypeName);
```

```
        // Display each method call parameter as name=value pairs.
        for(int i = 0; i < methodCall.ArgCount; i++)
        {
            Console.WriteLine("{0} = {1}", methodCall.GetArgName(i),
                methodCall.GetArg(i));
        }
    }
}
```

This example casts the incoming IMessage object to an IMethodCallMessage interface. Then it uses various IMethodCallMessage properties and methods to retrieve information about the method call contained in the message. Keep in mind that this is just a hypothetical example to demonstrate the IMethodCallMessage functionality. In the upcoming sections, you will learn how to actually intercept method call messages and interrogate them.

Understanding Aspect Oriented Programming

As shown in Listing 4-12, if you can intercept a method call while it is in transit from the caller to the target object, you can retrieve all of the core details of the message. The obvious question, however, is how could you apply this capability? Generally speaking, you can use it to implement a new style of programming called *Aspect Oriented Programming* (AOP).

Consider Figure 4-8, which shows the classical representation of an *n*-tier application with presentation, business, and data logic layers. In addition to solving the core business task, you may also need to handle issues such as logging, use tracking, security, exception handling, and so on. Furthermore, many of these are *cross-cutting concerns*; that is, they are issues that must be solved at every layer of the application. In Figure 4-8, these issues are encapsulated within the Common Services layer.

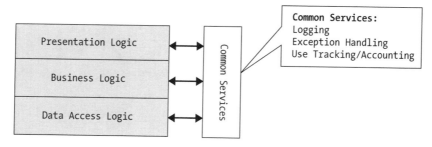

Figure 4-8. An n-tier application with cross-cutting concerns implemented in the Common Services layer

The typical solution for a cross-cutting concern is to build a utility class that provides the required functionality. For example, the code in Listing 4-13 uses the CustomException class to include the developer information within an exception.

Listing 4-13. Typical Exception-Handling Code

```
[DeveloperInfo("Homer", "hs@atomic.com")]
public class CustomerService
{
    public Customer GetCustomerByEmail(string email)
    {
        Customer cust = null;
        try
        {
            // Go get the customer
            cust = FetchTheCustomerFromDB(email);
        }
        catch(Exception e)
        {
            // This has nothing to do with getting a customer by email!
            CustomException custom = new CustomException(e, this);
            throw custom;
        }
        return cust;
    }
}
```

In this example, the CustomException class plays the role of a utility class by making it easy to retrieve the developer information and include it in the exception. Although it encapsulates most of the messy Reflection code to do this, you still must write the code that handles the general exception, creates the CustomException object, and raises the exception. And none of this is germane to the primary task at hand: retrieving a customer by e-mail. Instead, raising the custom exception is an *aspect* of the application that is tangential to the *aspect* of retrieving customer data.

The goal of AOP is to reduce the explicit interaction between aspects of the application. For example, the code in Listing 4-13 that raises the CustomException represents an explicit interaction between the exception aspect and the customer data aspect. The AOP philosophy holds that certain aspects can be encapsulated and transparently woven into the core logic of the application. In particular, cross-cutting concerns like exception handling and logging are excellent candidates for AOP-style implementations. If you applied AOP to Listing 4-13, you could remove all of the exception code, resulting in the code shown in Listing 4-14.

Listing 4-14. Listing 4-13 Refactored Using AOP

```
[DeveloperInfo("Homer", "hs@atomic.com")]  // Now, this is a context attribute!
public class CustomerService : ContextBoundObject
{
    public Customer GetCustomerByEmail(string email)
    {
        return FetchTheCustomerFromDB(email);
    }
}
```

Although it appears that the exception-handling code has simply been removed, it has, in fact, been moved into the DeveloperInfo attribute, which has been reimplemented as a context attribute. Also notice that the CustomerService class now derives from ContextBoundObject. Actually, a few additional modifications are working behind the scenes to make Listing 4-14 possible. These are detailed in the following sections, but before studying them, it is important to note the improvements represented in this example. The most obvious benefit is that AOP greatly simplifies the customer data retrieval aspect by removing the exception handling aspect from the code. This, in turn, results in a loose coupling between the aspects and a code base, which is much easier to maintain. For example, you can drastically change the implementation of the exception aspect without rewriting any other code.

Understanding the Context Sink Chain

As noted earlier, a runtime-generated proxy converts a method call made on a context-bound object into a message object and passes the message object to the context that contains the actual object. While crossing the context boundary, the message will pass through a variety of objects known as *message sinks*. Conceptually, these message sinks are linked together to form a chain of objects known as the *context sink chain*. When the message arrives at a given message sink, the message sink can execute any required interception logic, and then pass the message on to the next message sink in the chain.

Eventually, the last message sink hands the message to a runtime object called the *stack builder*. The stack builder converts the message back into a method call and invokes the method on the context-bound object. The method return value is also converted into a message and passed back through the same context sink chain in the reverse direction. This gives each message sink in the chain the opportunity to process the return value and execute any required postprocessing logic.

Examining Context Sink Chains

The context sink chain is divided into several different chains, each containing a different type of sink object. To describe each chain, let's follow a cross-context method call as it travels through the infrastructure. First, we need a class that is context bound. Recall from Chapter 3 that you can use the Synchronization attribute combined with the ContextBoundObject base class to define a context-bound type, as follows:

```
[Synchronization()]
public class MyContextBoundClass : ContextBoundObject
{ // ...
}
```

Now consider the following example:

```
MyContextBoundClass myBound = new MyContextBoundClass()
myBound.SomeMethod();
```

The first line in this example causes the runtime to create the object in a separate context and establish the entire context sink chain. It then generates a proxy and returns a reference to it from the new operator. The second line invokes a method on the proxy object and triggers the process described in the following paragraphs and illustrated in Figure 4-9.

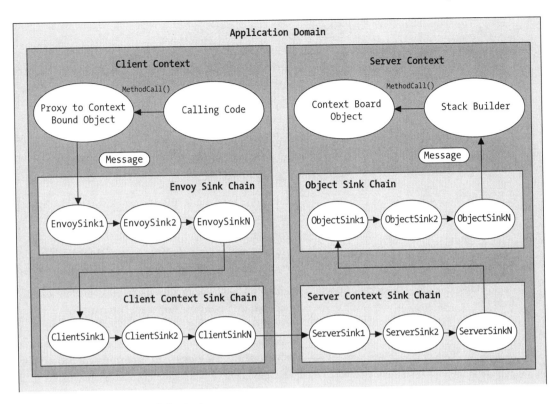

Figure 4-9. The context sink chains

First, when the SomeMethod() method is called, the proxy converts the method call to an IMessage object and passes the message to a series of sinks called the *envoy sink chain*. This chain is always present whenever making cross-context calls, and it executes in the caller's (or client) context. The last envoy sink passes the message to the *client context sink chain*. This chain also executes within the client context. However, the runtime builds this chain only if the method call originates from a context-bound object calling another context-bound object. The last client context sink passes the message to a cross-context channel, which carries the message over the context boundary and passes it to the server context.

Once in the server context, the message must first pass through the *server context sink chain*. The last server context sink in this chain passes the message to the *object sink chain*. Finally, the last object sink passes the message to the internal stack builder object, which invokes the message on the context-bound object.

It is possible to implement your own custom interception logic within a message sink and insert it into any of these context sink chains. Table 4-4 summarizes some of the differences between the sink chains and why you might choose one type over another.

Table 4-4. Context Sink Chains

Sink Chain	Executes In	Description
Envoy sink	Client context	Intercepts calls from any client to the context-bound object. Executes in the client context and can be used to validate calls before any other expensive marshaling is done.
Client sink	Client context	Intercepts all calls leaving the context of a context-bound object. You can use this chain to log all outgoing method calls.
Server sink	Server context	Intercepts all calls entering the context. The runtime establishes one server context sink chain that provides interception for any number of objects contained in the context. You can use this chain to provide per-context logging of incoming method calls.
Object sink	Server context	Intercepts all calls entering the context and invoked on a given object in the context. The runtime establishes one object sink chain for each object bound to the context. You can use this chain to provide per-object logging of incoming method calls.

Defining a Custom Message Sink

Regardless of the type of sink chain, all message sink objects implement the IMessageSink interface shown in Listing 4-15.

Listing 4-15. The IMessageSink Interface

```
public interface IMessageSink
{
    IMessageSink NextSink { get; }
    IMessage SyncProcessMessage(IMessage msg);
    IMessageCtrl AsyncProcessMessage(IMessage msg, IMessageSink replySink);
}
```

If you wish to add a custom message sink to any of the context sink chains, you must first define a class that implements this interface. Here are the minimal steps to create a message sink.

- Define a class that implements the `IMessageSink` interface.

- In the class, add a constructor that accepts a reference to the next message sink in the chain. Store this reference in an instance field.

- Implement the `NextSink` property to simply return the cached reference to the next message sink.

- Implement the `SyncProcessMessage()` method to perform any preprocessing on the given message before calling `SyncProcessMessage()` on the next message sink in the chain. Then perform any postprocessing on the returned `IMessage` object before returning it to the caller.

- Implement the `AsyncProcessMessage()` method to perform preprocessing and postprocessing on asynchronous calls.

To help clarify these steps, we will implement a custom message sink, called `DeveloperInfoSink`. This sink will work with the `DeveloperInfo` attribute to intercept exceptions rising from the context and replace each exception with a `CustomException` that includes the developer information along with the rest of exception details. The partial code is shown in Listing 4-16.

Listing 4-16. The DeveloperInfoSink Class Construction Code

```
public class DeveloperInfoSink : IMessageSink
{
    private IMessageSink mNextSink;
    private DeveloperInfoAttribute mDevInfo;

    public DeveloperInfoSink(IMessageSink nextSink,
        DeveloperInfoAttribute devInfo)
    {
        mNextSink = nextSink;
        mDevInfo = devInfo;
    }

    public IMessageSink NextSink
    {
        get {return mNextSink; }
    }
    // See Listing 4-17 for message processing logic
}
```

This code segment includes the sink construction logic and the `NextSink` property. When this sink is constructed, it is passed as a reference to the next sink in the context chain and a reference to a `DeveloperInfoAttribute` instance. The constructor stores both of these references in instance fields for later use. The read-only `NextSink` property simply returns the reference to the next sink.

This does beg the following question, however: Who creates this custom sink object? In the next section, you will see how a special type of context attribute constructs the sink, but for now, it is enough to understand that it will be constructed when required.

The most important method of any message sink is the `SyncProcessMessage()` method. This method takes a reference to an `IMessage` object that represents the original method call. You can use this object to investigate several different facts regarding the method call. For example, you can loop through all the passed arguments and log the entire method call to a file. However, keep in mind that `IMessage` objects are read-only. Therefore, if your preprocessing or postprocessing logic involves changing the message in any way, you must generate a new message object with the required updates. The `DeveloperInfoSink` class shown in Listing 4-17 demonstrates some of these techniques.

Listing 4-17. DeveloperInfoSink Message Processing Logic

```
public class DeveloperInfoSink : IMessageSink
{
    public IMessage SyncProcessMessage(IMessage msg)
    {
        msg = PreProcess(msg);
        IMessage returnMsg = mNextSink.SyncProcessMessage(msg);
        return PostProcess(msg, returnMsg);
    }

    private IMessage PreProcess(IMessage msg)
    {
        // No preprocessing required
        return msg;
    }
    private IMessage PostProcess(IMessage msg, IMessage returnMsg)
    {
        Console.WriteLine("PostProcessing");
        IMethodReturnMessage rm = (IMethodReturnMessage)returnMsg;
        if (rm.Exception != null)
        {
            rm = new ReturnMessage(new CustomException(rm.Exception, mDevInfo),
                (IMethodCallMessage)msg);
        }
```

```
        return rm;
    }

    public IMessageCtrl AsyncProcessMessage(IMessage msg, IMessageSink replySink)
    {
        // This sink only supports synchronous calls
        return null;
    }
}
}
```

This example implements SyncProcessMessage() by first passing the given IMessage object to the PreProcess() helper method. This helper method is really just a template for possible future preprocessing. In the case of DeveloperInfoSink, no preprocessing is necessary, so it simply returns the given IMessage object.

Next, SyncProcessMessage() invokes SyncProcessMessage() on the next message sink object in the chain. Each subsequent message sink does the same, until the method is executed on the target object. Then the return value is passed back through the context chain in reverse. Therefore, the return value from the SyncProcessMessage() call is actually an IMessage object representing the return value from the target method. The return message and the original method call message are then passed to the PostProcess() helper method for postprocessing.

The PostProcess() helper method demonstrates the usefulness of the interception mechanism. This method casts the return message to an IMethodReturnMessage interface and checks the Exception property. If the property is null, then no exception has occurred and the return message can be passed as is. However, if an exception has occurred, then this exception is used to construct a CustomException object similar to the one defined in Listing 4-10. Notice that the developer information is also passed to the CustomException constructor. Finally, the CustomException object and the original message object are used to construct a new ReturnMessage object. This new return message is returned to the client code, which can catch the exception and investigate the developer information.

Creating a Context Attribute and Context Property

Although DeveloperInfoSink is now fully implemented, it is useless unless you can somehow insert it into the context sink chain. To accomplish this, you must implement a custom context attribute and apply it to a class deriving from ContextBoundObject. In addition to serving as a standard custom attribute, the context attribute can provide the necessary logic to insert the custom sink into the context chain whenever the runtime creates an instance of its target class.

First and foremost, a context attribute is a custom attribute like any other created in this chapter, except that it implements the `IContextAttribute` interface, shown in Listing 4-18.

Listing 4-18. The IContextAttribute Interface

```
public interface IContextAttribute
{
    void GetPropertiesForNewContext(IConstructionCallMessage msg);
    bool IsContextOK(Context ctx, IConstructionCallMessage msg);
}
```

When the runtime creates a context-bound object, it iterates through each context attribute applied to the object's class and calls the `IsContextOk()` method while passing a reference to the current context. If any one of the context attributes returns `false`, then the runtime calls the `GetPropertiesForNewContext()` method on each of the context attributes and uses the results to construct a new context.

In the implementation of the `GetPropertiesForNewContext()` method, the context attribute is expected to use the provided constructor message (`IConstructionCallMessage`) to add a *context property* or properties to the new context. A context property is an object that implements (at the very least) the `IContextProperty` interface, shown in Listing 4-19.

Listing 4-19. The IContextProperty Interface

```
public interface IContextProperty
{
    string Name { get; }
    void Freeze(Context newContext);
    bool IsNewContextOK(Context newCtx);
}
```

When the runtime finishes creating the new context, it calls the `IsNewContextOk()` method on each context property. This allows the context property to investigate the new context and determine if it is acceptable. For example, the context property could check for conflicting properties in the same context and return `false` if any were found.

Ultimately, each context property in the context defines the behavior of the context because it acts as the factory for a message sink or sinks. During the construction of the context-bound object, the runtime attempts to cast each context property to the interfaces shown in Table 4-5. Compare this to Table 4-4 and notice that there is one of these interfaces for each type of context sink chain. If the cast is successful, the runtime invokes the associated factory method and inserts the returned message sink into the appropriate context sink chain.

Table 4-5. The Message Sink Factory Interfaces

Sink Factory Interface	Factory Method	Description
IContributeEnvoySink	GetEnvoySink()	The runtime inserts the returned message sink into the envoy sink chain.
IContributeClientContextSink	GetClientContextSink()	The runtime inserts the returned message sink into the client context sink chain.
IContributeServerContextSink	GetServerContextSink()	The runtime inserts the returned message sink into the server context sink chain.
IContributeObjectSink	GetObjectSink()	The runtime inserts the returned message sink into the object sink chain.

Deriving from the ContextAttribute Class

As the context attribute designer, you could implement two separate classes: one to play the role of the context attribute and another to be the context property. Of course, this would mean you would need to implement the IContextAttribute interface, the IContextProperty interface, and at least one of the message sink factory interfaces. However, the context attribute and the context property do not need to be a different class. In fact, it is often more convenient to have one class implement all these interfaces and serve as the context attribute, context property, and message sink factory.

Adding to this convenience is the ContextAttribute base class. This class provides default implementations of IContextAttribute and IContextProperty. Therefore, a class deriving from ContextAttribute needs to implement only one or more of the message sink factory interfaces to become a fully functional context attribute.

The ContextAttribute base class is demonstrated in Listing 4-20. This example upgrades the custom DeveloperInfo attribute used in earlier examples to a context attribute.

Listing 4-20. The DeveloperInfo Context Attribute

```
[AttributeUsage(AttributeTargets.Class, Inherited=true)]
public sealed class DeveloperInfoAttribute
    : ContextAttribute, IContributeObjectSink
{
    public DeveloperInfoAttribute(string name, string email)
        : base("DeveloperInfo")
    {
        mName = name;
        mEmail = email;
    }

    public DeveloperInfoAttribute(string name)
        :base("DeveloperInfo")
    {
        mName = name;
    }

    public IMessageSink GetObjectSink(MarshalByRefObject obj,
        IMessageSink nextSink)
    {
        return new DeveloperInfoSink(nextSink, this);
    }

    // Snipped properties, fields, and ToString method for brevity
}
```

In this example, notice the subtle change in the attribute's constructors. The ContextAttribute base class must be constructed with a provided context property name. This is just a friendly string name used by the runtime to identify and retrieve the context property. The constructors in this example simply pass a hard-coded value, "DeveloperInfo", to the ContextAttribute base class.

Although the ContextAttribute base class provides most of the implementation needed, it does not implement a message sink factory interface. So, in this example, the DeveloperInfo attribute implements the IContributeObjectSink interface to create and return a DeveloperInfoSink message sink. When the context is established, the runtime will add this custom sink to the object sink chain. Given the implementation of the DeveloperInfoSink message sink, this means that any exception raised from the context-bound object will be intercepted and replaced with a CustomException containing both the original exception and the developer information.

Testing the Custom Context Attribute

Now it's time to see what has been accomplished with all this extra context and interception logic. Remember, what initially prompted this discussion was the realization that the DeveloperInfo attribute was useful only if the class developer was careful to capture every system exception and replace it with a CustomException before raising it back to the client.

However, by making the DeveloperInfo attribute a context attribute, you can now leverage the built-in context-interception mechanisms to handle any system exception correctly. For example, consider the simple Demo class shown in Listing 4-21 and compare it with the previous example in Listing 4-11.

Listing 4-21. Using the DeveloperInfo Context Attribute

```
[DeveloperInfo("Homer", "hs@atomic.com", WorkPhone="555-5555")]
public class Demo : ContextBoundObject
{
    public void DemoMethod()
    {
        // Look ma! No exception handling!
        ForceException();
    }

    private void ForceException()
    {
        int zero = 0;
        int i = 5 / zero;
    }
}
```

Unlike the earlier Demo class, this class derives from ContextBoundObject and does not explicitly implement any exception handling. Instead, this will be managed by the custom DeveloperInfoSink message sink defined in Listing 4-17.

Finally, Listing 4-22 shows a couple of client code options for handling the exception raised from the Demo.DemoMethod() method. First, the client code captures the CustomException, uses it to display the developer information, and continues execution. The second section demonstrates what happens if the client code does not catch the exception.

Listing 4-22. Testing the DeveloperInfo Context Attribute

```
static void Main(string[] args)
{
    // Demo is created in separate context
    Demo d = new Demo();

    // Catch the exception
    try
    {
        d.DemoMethod();
    }
    catch(CustomException ce)
    {
        Console.WriteLine("\n** Begin Developer Info **");
        Console.WriteLine("Name: {0}", ce.DeveloperInfo.Name);
        Console.WriteLine("Email: {0}", ce.DeveloperInfo.Email);
        Console.WriteLine("Work Phone: {0}", ce.DeveloperInfo.WorkPhone);
        Console.WriteLine("Mobile Phone: {0}", ce.DeveloperInfo.MobilePhone);
        Console.WriteLine("** End Developer Info **\n");
    }

    // What happens with no try/catch?
    d.DemoMethod();
}
```

The output from Listing 4-22 is shown in Figure 4-10. Notice that even when the exception is not handled by the client, the developer information is included in the exception dump.

```
D:\Apress\Attributes\c4\Scratch\DeveloperInfoContext\Client\bin\Debug\Client.exe   _ □ ×
** Begin Developer Info **
Name: Homer
Email: hs@atomic.com
Work Phone: 555-5555
Mobile Phone:
** End Developer Info **


Unhandled Exception: DeveloperInfo.CustomException: Attempted to divide by zero.
 ---> System.DivideByZeroException: Attempted to divide by zero.
   at Client.Demo.ForceException() in d:\apress\attributes\c4\scratch\developeri
nfocontext\client\demo.cs:line 59
   at Client.Demo.DemoMethod() in d:\apress\attributes\c4\scratch\developerinfoc
ontext\client\demo.cs:line 19
   at System.Runtime.Remoting.Messaging.Message.Dispatch(Object target, Boolean
fExecuteInContext)
   at System.Runtime.Remoting.Messaging.StackBuilderSink.SyncProcessMessage(IMes
sage msg, Int32 methodPtr, Boolean fExecuteInContext)
   --- End of inner exception stack trace ---

Server stack trace:


Exception rethrown at [0]:
   at System.Runtime.Remoting.Proxies.RealProxy.HandleReturnMessage(IMessage req
Msg, IMessage retMsg)
   at System.Runtime.Remoting.Proxies.RealProxy.PrivateInvoke(MessageData& msgDa
ta, Int32 type)
   at Client.Demo.DemoMethod() in d:\apress\attributes\c4\scratch\developerinfoc
ontext\client\demo.cs:line 19
   at Client.ClientMain.Main(String[] args) in d:\apress\attributes\c4\scratch\d
eveloperinfocontext\client\main.cs:line 33
Developer Information:Name=Homer;Email=hs@atomic.com;Work Phone=555-5555;Mobile
Phone=
Press any key to continue
```

Figure 4-10. Listing 4-19 output

SOURCE CODE   *The complete code for the DeveloperInfo context attribute example is in Chapter4\DeveloperInfoContextAttribute.*

Revisiting AOP

You have now seen the power of AOP programming and the steps required to implement it. However, adopting AOP is not without risks. Before refactoring all of your applications to use AOP, consider the following points:

Early adoption: Although there has been a significant amount of study and work in the field of AOP, it is not a prevalent programming practice for business applications. AOP is truly bleeding edge; if you choose to implement an AOP solution, you will have few resources to consult for assistance.

Team buy-in: Few of us work in isolation or have the luxury of dictating a radical development paradigm like AOP. Therefore, you must convince management that AOP is viable for a given project, and you must educate your team members about the reasons for AOP, how it works, and how to implement it.

Performance: Using .NET's context-interception mechanism to implement AOP does have a negative impact on performance. The process of serializing the call into a message, passing it through the message sinks, deserializing the message, and finally invoking the method obviously takes much longer than a simple method call. Therefore, you must judiciously apply context interception and AOP to avoid a drastic decrease in application performance.

Multiple-aspect orchestration: The most common aspects are those that don't change the method call, such as a logging aspect. However, aspects that do modify the method call or cause other side effects can complicate matters, particularly if they are combined and used together. In this case, the order that the aspects are invoked may affect the outcome. For example, assume AspectA asserts a security credential required by AspectB. If AspectA executes before AspectB, then the call succeeds. However, if AspectB executes before AspectA, then the call fails due to the security issue.

Despite these risks, AOP offers exciting possibilities for developers who write and maintain frameworks for business applications. Although it may be a new concept for business programmers, it isn't completely untested. In fact, the roots of AOP go back to MTS and continue into COM+. Most recently, you can see the AOP philosophy applied again in the implementation of SOAP Extensions. Ultimately, only you can decide if the benefits of AOP outweigh the risks for a given application.

Conclusion

In this chapter, you learned many details regarding the creation and application of custom attributes, including the following:

- A custom attribute is simply a class that derives from the `Attribute` base class.

- A custom attribute is useful only to the extent that consuming code uses Reflection to discover the existence of the attribute and takes the appropriate action.

- A context attribute is a special type of custom attribute. It can implement two interfaces—IContextAttribute and IContextProperty—or it can derive from the ContextAttribute base class, which provides default implementations for these interfaces.

- A context property supplies the runtime with custom message sinks that it inserts into the context sink chain. These custom message sinks can then participate in interception of method calls as they flow across the context boundary.

In the next chapter, you will continue to apply these techniques by walking through the implementation of a checked exception mechanism for .NET (similar to Java's checked exception capability). This not only uses more custom attributes, but it also involves the creation of a custom compiler.

CHAPTER 5

Applying Custom Attributes

Up to this point, you've learned how attributes work inside and out. You've not only seen a lot of examples of out-of-the-box .NET attributes, but you've also explored how to create your own custom attributes. However, as with any development concept, the process will crystallize when you see a full-blown application that uses custom applications. That's what this chapter is all about.

In this chapter, we'll create an attribute that can be added to a method to tell the developer that the method may throw an exception. You'll see how this works in the Java language and how it can be applied in the .NET world through attributes. You'll gain insight into the CodeDOM classes to extend the compilation process, along with a custom library to inspect the underlying CIL to ensure that these dangerous methods are handled correctly.

Understanding Checked Exceptions in Java

It doesn't take a lot of .NET programming to find out that sometimes you need to add a try...catch block to a section of your code to save your application from an unexpected death. Exceptions occur as a result of a situation that the developer either did not expect or did not want to happen. For example, you may try to open a file via System.IO.File.Open(), but the file doesn't exist. Or you might try to open a connection to a database via a SqlConnection instance, but the database is down. Such circumstances need to be reported quickly to the developer to prevent the code from continuing.[1]

However, you may not know that when you call a particular method, you're running the risk of getting an exception. Consider the following code:

```
//  Assume that fictitiousfile.txt doesn't exist.
public void UseFile()
{
    FileStream file = File.Open("fictitiousfile.txt", FileMode.Open);
}
```

---

1. It would not be a pleasant situation if a developer tried to submit query after query if she couldn't get a database connection in the first place.

When `Open()` is invoked, the caller will receive `FileNotFoundException`. To defend against an unhandled exception, the code can be changed to this:

```
//  Assume that fictitiousfile.txt doesn't exist.
public void UseFile()
{
    try
    {
        FileStream file = File.Open("fictitiousfile.txt", FileMode.Open);
    }
    catch(FileNotFoundException fnfe)
    {
        //  Log the exception, send an e-mail to the developer, etc.
    }
}
```

The reason you know that `Open()` can throw `FileNotFoundException` is that the .NET SDK tells you so. However, take a look at this code:

```
//  Assume that fictitiousfile.zip doesn't exist.
public void UseThirdPartyAssembly()
{
    ZipStream file = ZippedFile.Open("fictitiousfile.zip", ZipFileMode.Open);
}
```

In this case, an assembly was purchased from a vendor to handle compressed files. Here, what will `Open()` do if the given file doesn't exist? You could check the vendor's documentation, but there is no guarantee that this documentation will tell you all of the exceptions that could occur when `Open()` is invoked.

In the Java world, things are a bit different. If `ZippedFile` were a Java class, and `Open()` had the potential of throwing `ZippedFileMissingException` somewhere within its implementation, `Open()` would need to be declared like this:

```
public ZipStream Open() throws ZippedFileMissingException
{
    //  Implementation goes here...
}
```

Notice the `throws` keyword in the method definition. This tells the Java compiler to error out if another method calls `Open()` without a `try...catch` block around the `Open()` invocation, where the `catch` block will catch `ZippedFileMissingException`. It will also error out if the calling method doesn't have the `throws` statement in its method definition.

It's a fact that the .NET Framework was not designed to support checked exceptions. Whether this is a good thing or a bad thing is subject for debate, but it's highly unlikely that such a mechanism will ever show up in .NET. However, it is possible to add checked exception support by creating a compiler that extends the C# compiler. The new compiler could look for unhandled exceptions and method invocations that are marked with a custom attribute. Let's take a look at how this could be done.

NOTE   *Our intention is* not *to re-create the checked exception mechanism from Java exactly; that is, our end result may not match the way the mechanism works in Java. The main goal is to demonstrate how you can extend the compilation process with metadata.*

Why Isn't the Checked Exception Mechanism in .NET?

When .NET became available to the public in its first beta cycle, many Java developers who saw the similarities between Java and C# wondered why checked exceptions were nowhere to be found. The issue has been discussed in depth. Here are just a few of the places you can find discussions regarding checked exceptions and .NET:

- http://www.mindview.net/Etc/Discussions/CheckedExceptions

- http://discuss.develop.com/archives/wa.exe?A2=ind0011A&L= DOTNET&P=R32820

- http://www.kuro5hin.org/story/2002/10/7/11507/3854

Regardless of our views on this topic, we strongly doubt that this mechanism will show up in .NET. This is because the .NET Framework is intended to support multiple languages, many of which do not have the notion of checked exceptions.

Granted, most of the .NET assemblies that will be created will be done in either C# or VB .NET. However, there are a number of languages that now have .NET compilers, like Eiffel (Eiffel for .NET), Smalltalk (S#), and Component Pascal, just to name a few. None of these languages have checked exceptions, and while it could have been possible to implement this mechanism via the attribute technique demonstrated in this chapter, we think the .NET designers decided that the majority wins. There are simply too many languages that do not support checked exceptions, and adding it in at the CLR level would have required every language and its related compilers that targeted the .NET platform to understand this notion.

Personally, we like the idea of checked exceptions (although we do see valid points on both sides of the issue). We've already been burned by calling a couple of methods within the .NET Framework that were not properly documented and getting unexpected exceptions. Although adding exception handling would have solved the problem, it's definitely not a cure-all. Including exception handling is not cheap from a performance standpoint, so it should be added to code only when needed. Therefore, knowing when a method is potentially dangerous without relying on documentation is a good thing. But it will probably never materialize in the CLR.

Implementing Checked Exceptions in .NET

To mimic checked exceptions in .NET, we need to create two items:

- An attribute so metadata can be associated with a method that may be dangerous

- A compiler that will look for these dangerous methods, along with methods that throw exceptions

The first item is fairly easy to create, but implementing the second one isn't as straightforward. Let's get the easier part done first.

Defining the Attribute

The first thing we need to do is create an attribute that can be attached to a method or a property. This attribute will need only one piece of information: the type of the exception. Furthermore, a developer should be able to use this attribute on a method more than once. Listing 5-1 shows what this attribute looks like in code.

Listing 5-1. Defining ThrowsAttribute

```
[AttributeUsage(AttributeTargets.Method |
    AttributeTargets.Property, AllowMultiple = true,
    Inherited = true)]
public sealed class ThrowsAttribute : Attribute
{
    private const string ERROR_NOT_SUBCLASS =
        "The given type is not an Exception type.";
    private const string PARAM_EXCEPTION_TYPE = "exceptionType";
    protected Type mExceptionType = null;
```

```
    private ThrowsAttribute() : base() {}

    public ThrowsAttribute(Type exceptionType) : base()
    {
        if(exceptionType == null)
        {
            throw new ArgumentNullException(PARAM_EXCEPTION_TYPE);
        }

        Type baseExType = typeof(Exception);
        if(exceptionType != baseExType &&
            exceptionType.IsSubclassOf(typeof(Exception)) == false)
        {
            throw new ArgumentException(ERROR_NOT_SUBCLASS,
                PARAM_EXCEPTION_TYPE);
        }

        this.mExceptionType = exceptionType;
    }

    public Type ExceptionType
    {
        get
        {
            return this.mExceptionType;
        }
    }
}
```

Let's review this definition. First, note that this attribute can be used only on methods and properties via the AttributeTargets enumeration values. Also, we set AllowMultiple to true, which allows a developer to define multiple exceptions that a method could throw, as the following code snippet demonstrates:

```
[Throws(typeof(FileNotFoundException))]
[Throws(typeof(UriFormatException))]
public void DangerousMethod() {}
```

The attribute itself is straightforward. The only restriction is that the type given must be an Exception type when a ThrowsAttribute attribute is declared. This check is done via a call to IsSubclassOf() on the given Type object.

Creating a Custom Compiler

Okay, the simple part is done. Now comes the hard part: implementing a compiler that will check our code for checked exception violations. To illustrate why this is a little difficult, consider the following code:

```
public class TestCheckedExceptions
{
    public void ShouldThrowException(bool throwIt)
    {
        if(throwIt == true)
        {
            throw new ArgumentException();
        }
    }

    [Throws(typeof(CustomException))]
    public void AlwaysThrowsException()
    {
        throw new ExtendedCustomException();
    }

    [Throws(typeof(ApplicationException)]
    public void CallMethods()
    {
        try
        {
            this.ShouldThrowException(false);
        }
        catch(ArgumentException ae)
        {
            this.AlwaysThrowException();
        }
    }
}

public class CustomException : ApplicationException
{
    //  Implementation goes here...
}

public class ExtendedCustomException : CustomException
{
    //  Implementation goes here...
}
```

Our compiler needs to detect the following situations:

- In ShouldThrowException(), the possibility exists that it could throw an ArgumentException instance. Therefore, the compiler should error out and inform the user that this method needs to be marked with ThrowsAttribute.

- In AlwaysThrowsException(), the possibility exists that it could throw an ExtendedCustomException instance. However, the method is marked with ThrowsAttribute, but it's using CustomException as the exception type. This should be considered as acceptable by the compiler, though, since ExtendedCustomException derives from CustomException.

- In CallMethods(), it first calls ShouldThrowException(), passing in false. Although this will never create an ArgumentException instance, the developer will need to fix ShouldThrowException() to have the correct ThrowsAttribute attribute attached to it. However, even when this is done, CallMethods() is still acceptable, because the catch block will catch the exception marked in ThrowsAttribute. There is still a problem, however, because an exception will occur in AlwaysThrowsException(). Since it is not caught and CallMethods() is not marked with the correct exception type, the compiler should error out and inform the user that this method needs to be marked with a ThrowsAttribute attribute that contains the correct exception type.

Essentially, we need to go through each method in a class and determine how many exceptions are thrown within the method, along with how many methods are called that are marked with one or more ThrowsAttribute attributes. A list of exceptions is generated from this search. Then we go through each of these exceptions and determine if it is caught by an exception block. If the exception isn't handled, the last thing we need to do is see if the method itself is marked with the right ThrowsAttribute attribute. If it isn't, our compiler will generate an error. Figure 5.1 shows a flow diagram of this processing.

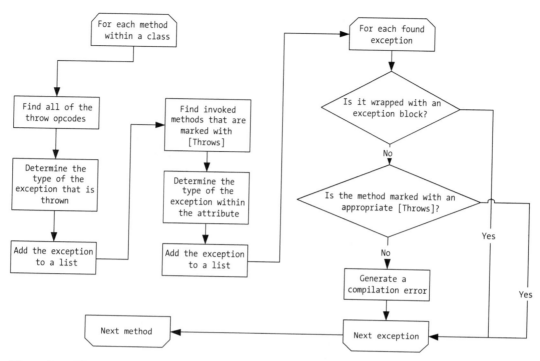

Figure 5-1. The process for finding unhandled exceptions

As you can guess, this isn't trivial to implement. This kind of parsing requires intimate details of a given method's internal information. Fortunately, there are classes available to ease the compiler implementation burden. The classes we'll use are part of the CodeDOM namespace (which is within the .NET Framework) and the FxCop tool created by Microsoft (which is freely available to any developer).

Implementing the Engine

We'll start our compiler implementation by creating a compiler that extends the C# compiler. This isn't as daunting as it sounds, because the .NET Framework has a number of relevant classes in the System.CodeDom namespace to make this rather easy to do. Essentially, we need to create two classes:

- One that extends CSharpCodeProvider, which is the factory class that generates the relevant compilers and parsers

- One that implements the ICodeCompiler interface and forwards most of the method implementations to the C# compiler instance

Figure 5-2 illustrates the design via a UML diagram.

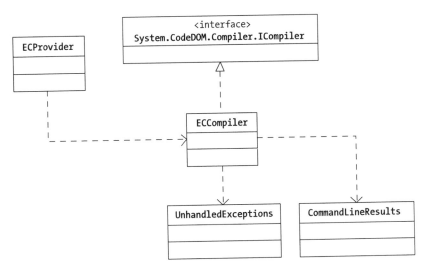

Figure 5-2. The design of the compiler engine

The intention is that a user will create an instance of our ECProvider and obtain an instance of our compiler via a call to CreateCompiler(). However, in CreateCompiler(), we give the user an instance of our compiler (ECCompiler), which uses the C# compiler. Listing 5-2 shows what it looks like in code (note that we're showing only the relevant details of these two classes in this code snippet).

Listing 5-2. Defining a Compiler and a Provider

```
public class ECProvider : CSharpCodeProvider
{
    private ECProvider() : base() {}

    public ECProvider(CommandLineResults cmdLineResults) : base()
    {
        if(cmdLineResults == null)
        {
            throw new ArgumentNullException(PARAM_CMD_LINE_RESULTS);
        }
```

```
            this.mCmdLineResults = cmdLineResults;
        }


        override public ICodeCompiler CreateCompiler()
        {
            return new ECCompiler(base.CreateCompiler(),
                this.mCmdLineResults);
        }
    }


    internal class ECCompiler : ICodeCompiler
    {
        private const string PARAM_COMPILER = "compiler";
        public const string ERROR_UNHANDLED_EXCEPTION_CODE = "EC0001";
        private const string ERROR_UNHANDLED_EXCEPTION_DESCRIPTION =
            "Method {0} in class {1} must state that " +
            "it may throw an exception of type {2}.";
        protected ICodeCompiler mCompiler = null;
        protected CommandLineResults mCmdLineResults = null;


        public ECCompiler(ICodeCompiler compiler, CommandLineResults cmdLineResults)
        {
            //   PRECONDITION: compiler != null.
            if(compiler == null)
            {
                throw new ArgumentNullException(PARAM_COMPILER);
            }


            this.mCompiler = compiler;
            this.mCmdLineResults = cmdLineResults;
        }
    }
}
```

Then the user will call one of the methods on the compiler object to create the assembly. As it stands, ICodeCompiler defines six methods for code compilation. To make things easier, we'll worry about only the calls to CompileAssemblyFromFileBatch() and let our wrapped C# compiler do its normal thing on any other ICodeCompiler calls. As soon as CompileAssemblyFromFileBatch() is invoked, we'll tweak the results a bit with our checked exception rules. For example, take a look at these two methods in ECCompiler:

```
public System.CodeDom.Compiler.CompilerResults
    CompileAssemblyFromFile(
    System.CodeDom.Compiler.CompilerParameters options, string fileName)
{
    return this.mCompiler.CompileAssemblyFromFile(options, fileName);
}

public System.CodeDom.Compiler.CompilerResults
    CompileAssemblyFromFileBatch(
    System.CodeDom.Compiler.CompilerParameters options, string[] fileNames)
{
    CompilerResults results = this.mCompiler.CompileAssemblyFromFileBatch(
        options, fileNames);
    CheckForFixup(this.mCmdLineResults);
    IsExceptionCatchingOK(this.mCmdLineResults, results);
    return results;
}
```

Granted, there are some items in this code that are not defined yet (like IsExceptionCatchingOK()), but you can see that when CompileAssemblyFromFileBatch() is called, we step in to do our own checks. Our custom compiler uses the other two classes: UnhandledExceptions and CommandLineResults. You'll see how UnhandledExceptions works in the "Finding Dangerous Methods and Thrown Exceptions" section later in this chapter. Here, we'll take a closer look at the CommandLineResults class.

It's more than likely that this compiler will be used from a command-line tool. We'll create this tool in the "Making a New Command-Line Compiler" section later in this chapter. However, since we know that we'll need to handle command-line parameters, we need to consider the parameter types of CompileAssemblyFromBatch().

Notice that the first argument is a CompilerParameters type. This class has a bunch of properties that need to be defined before the compiler is called, like IncludeDebugInformation and ReferencedAssemblies. Furthermore, if the user wants to compile an executable (EXE), the EXE file will end up in a temporary directory and not the one where the user invoked the compiler. To handle all of this in one class, we create the CommandLineResults class. Basically, this class takes the command-line arguments and translates them into a CompilerParameters type. Listing 5-3 shows a brief snippet of what this class does.

Listing 5-3. Defining CommandLineResults

```
public class CommandLineResults
{
    private const string SWITCH_SLASH = "/";
    private const string SWITCH_DASH = "-";
    private const string DEBUG_MINUS_OPTION = "debug-";
    private const string MAIN_OPTION = "main:";
    private const string NO_CONFIG_OPTION = "noconfig";
    private const string OUT_OPTION = "out:";
    private string[] mFiles = null;
    private bool mFixup = false;
    private CompilerParameters mParameters = null;

    public CommandLineResults(string[] args)
    {
        Initialize(args);
    }

    private void Initialize(string[] args)
    {
        bool useConfig = true;
        this.mParameters = new CompilerParameters();
        StringCollection filesCollection = new StringCollection();
        StringBuilder options = new StringBuilder();

        this.mParameters.GenerateExecutable = false;
        this.mParameters.GenerateInMemory = false;
        this.mParameters.IncludeDebugInformation = false;
        this.mParameters.TreatWarningsAsErrors = false;

        foreach(string arg in args)
        {
            int val = arg.IndexOf(SWITCH_SLASH);
            if(arg.IndexOf(SWITCH_DASH) == 0 ||
                arg.IndexOf(SWITCH_SLASH) == 0)
            {
                //  It's a C# switch - figure out if it maps to
                //  a property. If it doesn't, add it to options.
                if(arg.IndexOf(DEBUG_OPTION) == 1)
                {
```

```
                if(arg.IndexOf(DEBUG_MINUS_OPTION) == -1)
                {
                    this.mParameters.IncludeDebugInformation = true;
                }
            }
            else if(arg.IndexOf(MAIN_OPTION) == 1)
            {
                this.mParameters.MainClass =
                    arg.Substring(MAIN_OPTION.Length + 1);
            }
            else if(arg.IndexOf(OUT_OPTION) == 1)
            {
                this.mParameters.OutputAssembly =
                    arg.Substring(OUT_OPTION.Length + 1);
            }
            //  Keep going!
        }
    }
  }
}
```

We haven't shown the entire if statement because there are several else if tests. However, note that if the user is making an EXE, the Fixup property is set to true. The ECCompiler will do a post-build fixup to copy the EXE from the temporary location to the current directory if this property is true. This is done via a call to CheckForFixup():

```
private void CheckForFixup(CommandLineResults results)
{
    if(results.Fixup == true)
    {
        string currentLocation = results.Parameters.OutputAssembly;

        Assembly currentAssembly = Assembly.LoadFrom(
            currentLocation);

        string mainClass = currentAssembly.EntryPoint.DeclaringType.Name;

        string newFile = Path.Combine(Directory.GetCurrentDirectory(),
            string.Format("{0}.exe", mainClass));
```

```
        if(File.Exists(newFile) == true)
        {
            File.Delete(newFile);
        }

        File.Move(currentLocation, newFile);

        results.Parameters.OutputAssembly = newFile;
    }
}
```

 NOTE *If you take a look at* CommandLineResults *in the download-able code, you may wonder why there is a platform invoke to* GetCORSystemDirectory(). *This is necessary because the csc.exe tool will automatically reference the assemblies listed in the csc.rsp file located in the directory where the .NET Framework is installed. However, when you invoke the C#-based* CodeDOM *compiler, it isn't automatically referenced. Therefore, the* Initialize() *method will make that reference to the CSP file in the* CompilerOptions *property of the* CompilerParameters *object.*

Making a New Command-Line Compiler

Although developers could use our new compiler anywhere, they'll probably want to invoke the compiler from a command-line tool. This is handled by the ECCSC class, which simply uses our new ECProvider class. Listing 5-4 shows the details of the ECCSC's one and only method: Main().

Listing 5-4. Creating a Command-Line Interface to ECProvider

```
class ECCSC
{
    internal const string MESSAGE_OK = "EC compilation was successful.";
    internal const string MESSAGE_ERRORS = "EC compilation was unsuccessful.";
    internal const string MESSAGE_UNEXPECTED =
        "An unexpected exception occurred during EC compilation.";
    internal const string MESSAGE_UNKNOWN =
        "No results were returned from EC compilation.";
    internal const string MESSAGE_ERROR =
        "Error {0}\n\tCode: {1}\n\tDescription - {2}";
```

```
internal const int OK_STATUS = 0;
internal const int UNKNOWN_STATUS = 1;
internal const int UNHANDLED_ERROR_STATUS = 2;


static int Main(string[] args)
{
    int retVal = OK_STATUS;


    try
    {
        CodeDomProvider provider = new ECProvider(
            new CommandLineResults(args));
        ICodeCompiler compiler = provider.CreateCompiler();
        CommandLineResults cmdResults = new CommandLineResults(args);

        CompilerResults results = compiler.CompileAssemblyFromFileBatch(
            cmdResults.Parameters, cmdResults.Files);

        if(results != null)
        {
            if(results.Errors != null && results.Errors.Count > 0)
            {
                Console.WriteLine(MESSAGE_ERRORS);
                int errorCount = 1;

                foreach(CompilerError error in results.Errors)
                {
                    Console.WriteLine(string.Format(
                        MESSAGE_ERROR, errorCount,
                        error.ErrorNumber, error.ErrorText));
                    errorCount++;
                }
            }
            else
            {
                Console.WriteLine(MESSAGE_OK);
            }
        }
        else
        {
            retVal = UNKNOWN_STATUS;
            Console.WriteLine(MESSAGE_UNKNOWN);
        }
    }
```

```
        catch(Exception ex)
        {
            retVal = UNHANDLED_ERROR_STATUS;
            Console.WriteLine(MESSAGE_UNEXPECTED);
            Console.WriteLine(ex);
            Console.WriteLine(ex.StackTrace);
        }

        return retVal;
    }
}
```

Most of the code involves printing success or failure messages to the console window. The crux of the code is the four lines of code that are highlighted. The command-line interface lets ECCompiler do all of the work.

Parsing the CIL

Now we've come to the hardest part of the custom compiler. We need to actually parse the underlying CIL of each method in the assembly to determine if it passes our checked exception tests. This requirement is complicated by the fact that the .NET Framework does not provide any functionality to accomplish this task. The closest thing you can find is the System.Reflection.MethodBase class, but an instance of this class provides only metadata about the method it represents; it doesn't have a GetCIL() method. So how will we be able to find out what a method does?

 NOTE *Understanding CIL isn't that painful. For a full discussion, refer to* CIL Programming: Under the Hood of .NET *by Jason Bock (Apress, 2002).*

Fortunately, Microsoft has provided a free solution to the problem via the FxCop tool. This tool is used primarily by developers to check certain aspects of their assemblies to ensure that they follow certain guidelines. Figure 5-3 shows what this tool looks like when it is run.

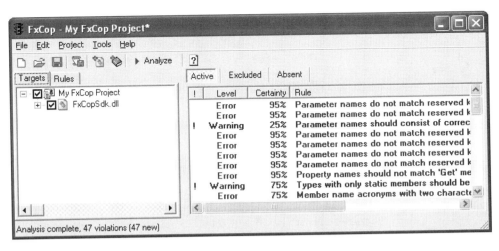

Figure 5-3. FxCop results

One interesting aspect of FxCop is that it allows you to define your own rules to enforce coding standards. To do this, the tool must be able to inspect a method's implementation, so the FxCop designers created a number of classes that traverse the CIL of a method. These classes can be found in the FxCopSdk.dll assembly, and they exist within the Microsoft.Tools.FxCop.Sdk.IL namespace. As you will see in the next two sections, these classes simplify the task of reading the CIL, allowing us to find our dangerous methods.

NOTE *To install the FxCop tool, visit* http://www.gotdotnet.com/ team/libraries. *Note that the code in this chapter uses the 1.21 version. Also, be aware that when you reference FxCopSdk.dll, it needs the NativeServices.dll file within the same directory to function properly. NativeServices.dll is an old-fashioned DLL in the sense that it is not a .NET assembly; it contains exported functions that are used by some of the classes in FxCopSdk.dll. Finally, there is no documentation for the FxCopSdk assembly, so using it can be a little cumbersome because you need to figure out what its classes can do. In our opinion, though, it's definitely worth the R&D time!*

Finding Dangerous Methods and Thrown Exceptions

The first thing we need to do after the C# compiler creates the assembly is to find each type within that assembly and look at all the methods it contains. Each method's CIL must then be inspected to find methods that are marked with the ThrowsAttribute or have the throw opcode somewhere within the opcodes. This is done in the IsExceptionCatchingOK() method within the ECCompiler class, which is shown in Listing 5-5.

Listing 5-5. Checking for Checked Exceptions

```
private bool IsExceptionCatchingOK(CommandLineResults cmdResults,
    CompilerResults results)
{
    bool retVal = true;

    Assembly newAssembly = results.CompiledAssembly;
    Type[] assemblyTypes = newAssembly.GetTypes();

    foreach(Type t in assemblyTypes)
    {
        BindingFlags methodBinding = BindingFlags.Public |
            BindingFlags.NonPublic | BindingFlags.Instance |
            BindingFlags.Static;

        MethodInfo[] typeMethods = t.GetMethods(methodBinding);

        if(typeMethods != null && typeMethods.Length > 0)
        {
            foreach(MethodInfo mi in typeMethods)
            {
                UnhandledExceptions uEx = new UnhandledExceptions(mi);

                if(uEx.ExceptionList.Count > 0)
                {
                    retVal = false;

                    foreach(Type exType in uEx.ExceptionList)
                    {
                        results.Errors.Add(new CompilerError(
                            newAssembly.Location,
                            0, 0, ERROR_UNHANDLED_EXCEPTION_CODE,
                            string.Format(ERROR_UNHANDLED_EXCEPTION_DESCRIPTION,
                            mi.Name, t.Name, exType.Name)));
                    }
                }
            }
        }
    }

    return retVal;
}
```

This method delegates most of the hard work to an UnhandledExceptions object. The primary job of IsExceptionCatchingOK() is to iterate through each MethodInfo object from each Type object in the assembly. Then it adds new CompilerError objects to the Errors collection based on what the UnhandledExceptions object reports, which can be used by a client of our compiler to determined what went wrong during compilation. The UnhandledExceptions object has one constructor that takes a MethodInfo instance. Within the constructor, it will find all of the exceptions that are not handled by the method and that are not marked with ThrowsAttribute. These exceptions are stored in an ArrayList, which is exposed via the ExceptionList property. Let's examine this constructor to see where the FxCop classes are used.

```
public class UnhandledExceptions
{
    private const string PARAM_TARGET_METHOD = "targetMethod";
    private const int MAX_OPCODE_SIZE = 4;
    protected ArrayList mExceptionList = new ArrayList();
    protected MethodInfo mTargetMethodInfo = null;
    protected Method mTargetMethod = null;
    protected byte[] mCIL = null;

    private UnhandledExceptions() : base() {}

    public UnhandledExceptions(MethodInfo targetMethod) : base()
    {
        // PRECONDITION: targetMethod != null.
        if(targetMethod == null)
        {
            throw new ArgumentNullException(PARAM_TARGET_METHOD);
        }

        this.mTargetMethodInfo = targetMethod;
        this.mTargetMethod = Method.GetMethod(targetMethod.DeclaringType.Module,
                this.mTargetMethodInfo);
        this.mCIL = this.mTargetMethod.GetILByteStream();
        this.FindUnhandledExceptions();
    }

    // Helper methods go here.
}
```

As you'll see when we dive into FindUnhandledExceptions(), we'll need a Method instance (note that the Method class definition comes from the FxCop library), along with the underlying CIL. Therefore, we translate the MethodInfo object into a `Method` via `GetMethod()`, and then we get the CIL into a byte array from `GetILByteStream()`. Both of these values are stored in instance fields so the instance methods always have access to them.

Once we have our instance fields set up, we can dive into `FindUnhandledExceptions()`, which is where the FxCop magic really kicks in. The method is a little lengthy, so we'll break it up into manageable chunks. Listing 5-6 shows the start.

Listing 5-6. Getting the Exceptions from the Method Implementation

```
protected void FindUnhandledExceptions()
{
    Hashtable methodExMarks = this.GetExceptionMarks();
    bool hasHandlers = true;

    if(methodExMarks.Count > 0)
    {
```

We're going to need to keep track of where dangerous code exists within a method, so we'll use a `Hashtable` instance to mark these locations. Remember that we need to find when exceptions are thrown and when methods that are marked with `ThrowsAttribute` are called. Furthermore, a method can have more than one `ThrowsAttribute` instance on it, so whenever we find one of these marked methods, we need to keep a list of the possible exceptions it can throw. This is the responsibility of `GetExceptionMarks()`. This method is also fairly long, so we'll break it up into two discussions. Listing 5-7 illustrates how thrown exceptions are tracked down.

Listing 5-7. Finding Thrown Exceptions in a Method Implementation

```
protected Hashtable GetExceptionMarks()
{
    Hashtable retVal = new Hashtable();

    ProgramStepCollection ps = this.mTargetMethod.DataFlow;
    int cilStart = 0;
    ArrayList methodExceptions = null;
```

```
if(ps != null && ps.Count > 0)
{
    //  Loop through the CIL and find out
    //  where the method calls and exceptions are.
    for(int i = 0; i < ps.Count; i++)
    {
        ProgramStep p = ps[i];

        if(p.Operation.Flow == ControlFlow.Throw)
        {
            //  Mark it.
            if(retVal.ContainsKey(cilStart) == true)
            {
                methodExceptions = (ArrayList)retVal[cilStart];
            }
            else
            {
                methodExceptions = new ArrayList();
                retVal.Add(cilStart, methodExceptions);
            }

            //  Find out what the exception is.
            if(p.Stacks != null && p.Stacks.Count > 0)
            {
                StackPossible currentStack = (StackPossible)p.Stacks[0];

                if(currentStack.Elements != null &&
                    currentStack.Elements.Count > 0)
                {
                    StackElement exOnStack =
                        (StackElement)currentStack.Elements.Peek();
                    Type exType = Type.GetType(
                        exOnStack.TypeName, false, false);

                    if(exType != null)
                    {
                        methodExceptions.Add(exType);
                    }
                }
            }
        }
    }
```

The DataFlow collection from the Method instance contains a list of ProgramStep objects, which represent the CIL opcodes as well as their associated operand data, if any exists. To illustrate what we mean by this, Figure 5-4 shows a method with the byte code data included, displayed in ILDasm.

```
ThrowsAttribute::.ctor : void(class [mscorlib]System.Type)              _ □ ×
.method /*0600001B*/ public hidebysig specialname rtspecialname
        instance void  .ctor(class [mscorlib/* 23000001 */]System.Type/*
// SIG: 20 01 01 12 2D
{
  // Method begins at RVA 0x2f18
  // Code size       84 (0x54)
  .maxstack  3
  .locals /*1100002F*/ init ([0] class [mscorlib/* 23000001 */]System.Ty|
  IL_0000:   /* 02  |                       */ ldarg.0
  IL_0001:   /* 14  |                       */ ldnull
  IL_0002:   /* 7D  | (04)000025            */ stfld       class [mscorlib/* 2
  IL_0007:   /* 02  |                       */ ldarg.0
  IL_0008:   /* 28  | (0A)00007E            */ call        instance void [msco
  IL_000d:   /* 03  |                       */ ldarg.1
  IL_000e:   /* 2D  | 0B                    */ brtrue.s    IL_001b
```

Figure 5-4. Methods in ILDasm

As you can see, some of the opcodes (like stfld) have operand data, and others (like ldnull) do not have this data. Fortunately, the ProgramStep class separates the two rather nicely for us via the Operation and Operand properties.

Returning to the code in Listing 5-7, to find a throw opcode, we need to inspect the Flow property on the ProgramStep object. This makes it extremely easy to determine the opcode code by comparing it to an enumeration value, rather than needing to know the exact values of every CIL opcode. The if statement is handling the case when a method throws an exception[2] by checking the Flow type to see if it's equal to the ControlFlow.Throw value. If it is, we need to mark this location in the CIL via methodExceptions. Since a throw opcode can throw only one exception, the corresponding ArrayList will contain only one exception type. But how do we find out what the exception type is?

Again, the FxCop classes come to the rescue. The Stacks property contains a StackPossible instance that we can use to look at what is currently on the CIL execution stack. Because the exception instance must be pushed onto the stack before the throw opcode, a call to Peek() will give us a StackElement instance, which will tell us the type of the exception on the stack via the TypeName property.

If the ProgramStep type isn't a Throw operation, we need to check for method invocations, because we need to check their metadata and see if any ThrowsAttribute attributes are associated with that called method. If there are, we need to see if the current method is handling it properly. Listing 5-8 completes the implementation of GetExceptionMarks() started in Listing 5-7.

---

2. Remember that, at this point, we're not figuring out if the exception is unhandled; we're just recording this fact. We'll make the determination if it's unhandled later on.

Listing 5-8. Finding Methods Calls Marked with ThrowsAttribute

```
else if(p.Operation.Flow == ControlFlow.Call)
{
    if(p.RawOperand is uint && ((uint)p.RawOperand > 0))
    //  It should be!
    {
        MethodBase rGetMethod = typeof(Method).GetMethod(
            "GetMethod", BindingFlags.NonPublic | BindingFlags.Static);

        Method mCalled = (Method)rGetMethod.Invoke(null, new object[]
            {this.mTargetMethod.AssemblyName,
            this.mTargetMethod.ModuleName, (uint)p.RawOperand});

        if(mCalled != null)
        {
            MethodBase mCalledBase = mCalled.MethodBase;

            if(mCalledBase != null)
            {
                //  Check to see if the method has been flagged with
                //   our custom [Throws] attribute
                object[] throwsAttribs =
                    mCalledBase.GetCustomAttributes(
                    typeof(ThrowsAttribute), true);

                if(throwsAttribs != null &&
                    throwsAttribs.Length > 0)
                {
                    if(retVal.ContainsKey(cilStart) == true)
                    {
                        methodExceptions = (ArrayList)retVal[cilStart];
                    }
                    else
                    {
                        methodExceptions = new ArrayList();
                        retVal.Add(cilStart, methodExceptions);
                    }

                    foreach(ThrowsAttribute throws in throwsAttribs)
                    {
                        methodExceptions.Add(throws.ExceptionType);
                    }
```

```
                    }
                }
            }
        }
    }

        cilStart += p.Length;
    }
}

    return retVal;
}
```

The biggest trick here is to convert the token value that represents the called method into a `MethodInfo` object so we can search its associated attributes. First, we pass the token that is stored in the `Operand` field as a `uint` to `GetMethod()` to get the method that is being invoked. Then we use the `MethodBase` property to get us back to the Reflection API, where we can look at the method's attributes. If there are any `ThrowsAttribute` attributes with this method, the exception types are extracted and added to a new `ArrayList`, which will be stored in the `Hashtable` at this point in the CIL stream.

Notice that before we move onto the next `ProgramStep`, we increase the size of `cilStart` appropriately. `ProgramStep` objects can vary in size, and we'll need to know where our dangerous methods and `throw` opcodes are when we try to determine if they leak (covered in the next section).

NOTE *You may be wondering why we're using Reflection to invoke the static* `GetMethod()` *method on the* `Method` *class. When this compiler was first written, an earlier version of the FxCop SDK assembly was used (1.091), and this method was* `public`. *Version 1.21 changed its accessibility to* `assembly`. *Therefore, the only way to call it was to use Reflection (because there was no other* `public` *method available that duplicated the functionality that* `GetMethod()` *provided in the SDK, this was the only feasible workaround).*

Remember that the main goal here is to find thrown exceptions or methods that are marked with `ThrowsAttribute`. We still haven't determined if the current method leaks those exceptions, but that is what the next section is all about.

Checking for Leaked Exceptions

Whew! That's a lot of work to do just to find the dangerous parts of a method. But we're not finished. Now we need to look at each `ArrayList` element within the `Hashtable` returned by `GetExceptionMarks()` and determine if any of them can leak out to the caller. If they can, our method better be marked with `ThrowsAttribute`, or the compilation will fail. Fortunately, the FxCop designers have made it rather easy for us to determine if an exception will leak, by supplying the `EHClause` object. But before we see how this object works, let's take a quick detour to see how exceptions are mapped out in CIL. Consider the following method:

```
public void SampleMethod()
{
    try
    {

    }
    catch(ArgumentException ae)
    {
        try
        {

        }
        finally
        {

        }
    }
}
```

If we use ILDasm to get the implementation of the method, we'll see something like this:

```
.method public hidebysig instance void  SampleMethod() cil managed
{
  // Code size       9 (0x9)
  .maxstack  1
  .locals init ([0] class [mscorlib]System.ArgumentException ae)
  IL_0000:  leave.s     IL_0008
  IL_0002:  stloc.0
  IL_0003:  leave.s     IL_0006
  IL_0005:  endfinally
  IL_0006:  leave.s     IL_0008
```

```
IL_0008:  ret
IL_0009:
// Exception count 2
.try IL_0003 to IL_0005 finally handler IL_0005 to IL_0006
.try IL_0000 to IL_0002 catch [mscorlib]System.ArgumentException
   handler IL_0002 to IL_0008
} // end of method ETest::SampleMethod
```

NOTE   *There are two things to note about this CIL generated from ILDasm. First, you need to compile the* SampleMethod() *in debug mode; otherwise, the C# compiler sees that it really does nothing and it won't put anything in the method. Second, make sure you have the Expand try/catch block menu option on the View menu turned off.*

Note that try...catch blocks are basically stored as checkpoints in the CIL. They tell you where the try, catch, and finally blocks start and end. The EHClause class tells you how the exception checkpoints are mapped out via the TryOffset, TryLength, HandlerOffset, and HandlerLength properties. Figure 5-5 illustrates how this method is laid out and what the EHClause fields would contain (note that the offset values are zero-based).

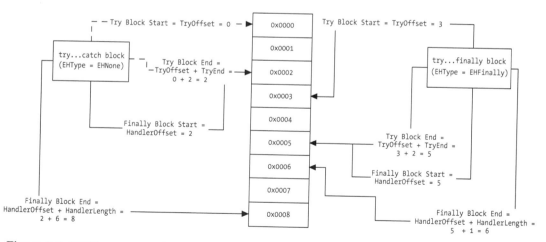

Figure 5-5. EHClause mapping

We can use EHClause class instances to determine if an exception can leak from the method. Essentially, our task is to take the list of the exceptions that can leak and determine if they're within a try...catch block that will handle that exception, which is where EHClause comes into play. Of course, as Figure 5-5 demonstrates, exception handlers can be embedded within other exception handlers, so the way to figure this out isn't trivial, but the EHClause class makes it manageable. Let's see how we do this by getting back to the implementation of FindUnhandledExceptions(), which is continued from Listing 5-6 in Listing 5-9.

Listing 5-9. Getting the EHClauses in FindUnhandledExceptions()

```
ArrayList exHandlers = this.mTargetMethod.RetrieveEHClauses();

if(exHandlers != null && exHandlers.Count > 0)
{
    for(int i = exHandlers.Count - 1; i >= 0; i--)
    {
        EHClause cTest = (EHClause)exHandlers[i];

        if(cTest.Type != EHClauseTypes.EHNone)
        {
            exHandlers.Remove(cTest);
        }
    }

    if(exHandlers.Count > 0)
    {
```

The RetrieveEHClauses() method gives us an ArrayList containing all of the EHClauses objects within the method. Now if we have exception handlers, we need to examine only those where the Type property is equal to EHClauseTypes.EHNone. The name of this enumeration may confuse matters at first, because it appears that we're looking for blocks that have no exception handling. Essentially, EHNone means that these are try blocks with catch blocks, which are the ones we care about.[3] After we parse the list, if we still have handlers, we can go through our found exceptions and see if the handlers will stop them from leaking to the caller, as shown in Listing 5-10.

---

3. For example, a try...finally block will automatically leak a thrown exception that occurs within the try block, so we don't need to check the block to see if it can handle an exception.

Listing 5-10. Checking for Leaked Exceptions in FindUnhandledExceptions()
Using EHClause Instances

```
foreach(object key in methodExMarks.Keys)
{
    uint keyValue = (uint)((int)key);
    ArrayList foundExceptions = (ArrayList)methodExMarks[key];
    foreach(Type foundExType in foundExceptions)
    {
        bool areAllTryBlocksProcessed = false;
        bool isHandled = false;
        int maxDistance = this.mCIL.Length;
        int minDistance = -1;

        do
        {
            bool foundOneHandler = false;
            foreach(EHClause clause in exHandlers)
            {
                uint tryEnd = clause.TryOffset + clause.TryLength;
                if(keyValue >= clause.TryOffset &&
                    keyValue <= tryEnd)
                {
                    int distance = Math.Abs((int)clause.TryOffset -
                        (int)keyValue) +
                        Math.Abs((int)tryEnd - (int)keyValue);
                    if(distance <= maxDistance && distance > minDistance)
                    {
                        foundOneHandler = true;
                        maxDistance = distance;
                        Type handlerEx = Type.GetType(
                            ILServices.GetNameForToken(
                            this.mTargetMethod.ModuleName,
                            clause.ClassTokenOrFilterOffset));

                        if(foundExType == handlerEx ||
                            foundExType.IsSubclassOf(handlerEx))
                        {
                            isHandled = true;
                            areAllTryBlocksProcessed = true;
                            break;
                        }
                    }
                }
            }
        }
```

```
            if(foundOneHandler == true)
            {
                minDistance = maxDistance;
            }
            else
            {
                areAllTryBlocksProcessed = true;
            }
        } while(areAllTryBlocksProcessed == false);

        if(isHandled == false)
        {
            this.CheckExceptionTypeInThrowsAttribute(foundExType);
        }
    }
}
```

This section of code iterates through our found exceptions and determines if any are not handled by exception handlers. To do this, we iterate through the EHClauses objects to see if the location of the exception in the CIL lies within the try block. If it does, we need to make sure it's the innermost one, which is what the distance variable is for.

Exception blocks can contain other exception blocks, so that is why we have a do loop. If we're in the try block, then we check the distance variable against the maxDistance value to ensure we're in the innermost block.[4] If we are there, we need to get the type of the exception that the catch block will handle. The type token is stored in the ClassNameOrFilterOffset property. This value can be translated into the type name for Type.GetType() via a call to GetNameForToken() on the ILServices class. If the catch block handles the found exception, we're finished with this exception, so we can stop iterating through the EHClause objects. If it's never handled, we'll break out of the loop.

Once we're out of the loop, we check to see if it's a leaked exception by inspecting the isHandled variable. If it is, the final (and most important) thing we need to do is to see if the current method states that it can throw this exception via the CheckExceptionTypeInThrowsAttribute() method:

---

4. Of course, try blocks can have multiple catch blocks, so we need to make sure we don't skip over those EHClauses objects where the distance value is going to be same. That is why we use a less-than-or-equal-to check.

```
protected void CheckExceptionTypeInThrowsAttribute(Type exceptionType)
{
    bool isMarked = false;

    object[] currentThrowsAttribs = this.mTargetMethodInfo.GetCustomAttributes(
        typeof(ThrowsAttribute), true);

    if(currentThrowsAttribs != null &&
        currentThrowsAttribs.Length > 0)
    {
        foreach(ThrowsAttribute currentThrows in currentThrowsAttribs)
        {
            if(exceptionType == currentThrows.ExceptionType ||
                exceptionType.IsSubclassOf(currentThrows.ExceptionType))
            {
                isMarked = true;
                break;
            }
        }
    }

    if(isMarked == false)
    {
        if(this.mExceptionList.Contains(exceptionType) == false)
        {
            this.mExceptionList.Add(exceptionType);
        }
    }
}
```

In this method, we check the attributes on our current method for
ThrowsAttribute instances. If we have any, we check their associated exception
types to see if the method is marked appropriately. If we don't have any attributes or we don't have the correct one, the leaked exception is added to the
mExceptionList, which means that the compilation process will error out.

Listing 5-11 finishes the implementation of FindUnhandledExceptions().

Listing 5-11. Finishing FindUnhandledExceptions()

```
else
{
    hasHandlers = false;
}
```

```
    }
    else
    {
        hasHandlers = false;
    }

    if(hasHandlers == false)
    {
        //  ALL of the found exceptions from GetExceptionMarks()
        //  must be marked by this method, or it's a compilation error
        foreach(object key in methodExMarks.Keys)
        {
            uint keyValue = (uint)key;
            ArrayList foundExceptions = (ArrayList)methodExMarks[key];
            foreach(Type foundEx in foundExceptions)
            {
                this.CheckExceptionTypeInThrowsAttribute(foundEx);
            }
        }
    }
}
```

If the method doesn't have any exception handlers, or none of the try blocks have catch blocks, we can trickle down to the simplistic case where we check all of the found exceptions against the method's attribute list.

NOTE   *If you take a look at the* CodeDomProvider *class, you'll notice that there's a* CreateParser() *method that returns an* ICodeParser-*based object. The interesting thing about this is that it looks like you could give the* Parse() *method a C# code file, and you would get a CodeDOM representation of the code. Therefore, we could have done the checked exception testing before the assembly was created. Why wasn't this approach taken? Because* CreateParser() *always returns* null! *Currently, no parser exists for any of the common .NET languages.*

Putting the ECCSC Compiler into Action

To finish the example, let's create a simple test .cs file where we can invoke eccsc.exe to see what it does. Our simple.cs file contains the following two classes:

```
using System;
using ECFramework;

public class ExceptionRiddledClass
{
    [Throws(typeof(ArgumentException))]
    public void DangerousMethod() {}

    public void InnocentMethod()
    {
        throw new InvalidCastException();
    }
}

public class TestClass
{
    public void UnmarkedMethod()
    {
        ExceptionRiddledClass erc = new ExceptionRiddledClass();
        erc.InnocentMethod();
    }

    [Throws(typeof(SystemException))]
    public void MarkedMethod()
    {
        ExceptionRiddledClass erc = new ExceptionRiddledClass();
        erc.DangerousMethod();
    }
}
```

Before we get to the results of eccsc.exe, think about what the compiler should do when it sees this code. Consider what exceptions may be thrown and which methods are marked as dangerous. This will help to check that the compiler does what we want it to do!

Okay, let's give the compiler a whirl. Run the following command:

```
eccsc /target:library /r:ECFramework.dll Simple.cs
```

You should see this as the result:

```
EC compilation was unsuccessful.
Error 1
        Code: EC0001
        Description - Method InnocentMethod in class ExceptionRiddledClass must
state that it may throw an exception of type System.InvalidCastException.
```

Cool! Our compiler saw that InnocentMethod() throws an InvalidCastException, and InnocentMethod() is marked appropriately.

Let's change InnocentMethod() so it has the correct ThrowsAttribute attribute on it:

```
[Throws(typeof(InvalidCastException))]
public void InnocentMethod()
{
    throw new InvalidCastException();
}
```

Now when the compiler is run, we'll get another error:

```
EC compilation was unsuccessful.
Error 1
        Code: EC0001
        Description - Method UnmarkedMethod in class TestClass must state that it
may throw an exception of type System.InvalidCastException.
```

Again, this is what we want to see. Since we just marked InnocentMethod() as not being so innocent anymore, our code in UnmarkedMethod() is now bad.

We can fix the code in two ways. The first solution is to simply tag the method with ThrowsAttribute:

```
[Throws(typeof(InvalidCastException))]
public void UnmarkedMethod()
{
    ExceptionRiddledClass erc = new ExceptionRiddledClass();
    erc.InnocentMethod();
}
```

The other solution is to put exception handling into the method itself, like this:

```
public void UnmarkedMethod()
{
    ExceptionRiddledClass erc = new ExceptionRiddledClass();

    try
    {
        erc.InnocentMethod();
    }
    catch(InvalidCastException ice) {}
}
```

Either approach will give us the following (desired) output when the compilation is run.

```
EC compilation was successful.
```

 SOURCE CODE *The code for these examples is in Chapter5\ECFramework, Chapter5\ECCSC, and Chapter5\ECSimpleTest.*

Conclusion

In this chapter, you learned about the following:

- Defining attributes that can be used during compilation

- How to create a custom compiler

- Parsing CIL via FxCop to determine if a method has the correct checked exception metadata

In this book, you've learned how attributes work in .NET and what metadata can do to your programs. You've seen how attributes are defined and why they are useful in certain situations. Attributes usually don't convey a ton of information, and it's fairly easy to create your own, but the necessary infrastructure you need to implement to make them useful isn't always trivial.

We hope that this book has helped you understand .NET attributes and now you have a better idea of when to use them. Happy metadata coding!

APPENDIX

Physical Representation of Metadata

EVEN THOUGH IT'S USUALLY not necessary to know the details of the metadata format in an assembly, we think it's educational to spend some time studying the attribute's byte array. You'll know how to interpret the metadata at a low level and be able to determine if a compiler is acting flaky when it stores metadata.[1] Furthermore, if you're a compiler writer, it's critical to know the ins and outs of the format. Therefore, in this appendix, we'll break down an attribute's byte array and see how it works.[2]

To start, let's create a custom attribute called TestAttribute, which we'll use to look at attribute byte arrays. Listing A-1 contains all of the code.

Listing A-1. Defining TestAttribute

```
namespace AttributeFormatting
{
    [AttributeUsage(AttributeTargets.Class)]
    public class TestAttribute : Attribute
    {
        protected int[] mIntArray = null;
        protected string mString = string.Empty;
        protected byte mByte = 0;
        public string mPublicString = string.Empty;

        protected TestAttribute() : base() {}

        public TestAttribute(string stringData, int[] intData) : base()
        {
            this.mIntArray = intData;
            this.mString = stringData;
        }
    }
```

---

1. A somewhat unlikely scenario, but compilers are not perfect.
2. You can find all of the gory details on the custom attribute serialization format in Sections 22.3 and 21.10 in Partition II.

```
        public byte ByteData
        {
            get
            {
                return this.mByte;
            }
            set
            {
                this.mByte = value;
            }
        }

        public string StringData
        {
            get
            {
                return this.mString;
            }
        }

        public int[] IntegerData
        {
            get
            {
                return this.mIntArray;
            }
        }
    }
}
```

Now let's apply TestAttribute to its only valid target, a class.

```
[TestAttribute("My string data.", new int[] {2, 3},
    ByteData = 22)]
public class TestClass {}
```

When a constructor is used on an attribute that takes one or more arguments, or if a no-argument constructor is used along with one or more named parameters, the information that was passed into the constructor parameters or named parameters needs to be stored. This will allow code that uses Reflection to read that metadata. Listing A-2 shows what that information looks like when you open the assembly in ILDasm.

Listing A-2. Attribute Byte Format

```
.custom instance void
  AttributeFormatting.TestAttribute::.ctor(string, int32[]) =
  ( 01 00 0F 4D 79 20 73 74 72 69 6E 67 20 64 61 74   // ...My string dat
    61 2E 02 00 00 00 02 00 00 00 03 00 00 00 01 00   // a..............
    54 05 08 42 79 74 65 44 61 74 61 16 )             // T..ByteData.
```

The first 2 bytes are 0x01 and 0x00. This will always be the case for every attribute array, because they all must start with a 16-bit prolog value equal to 0x0001. However, this may seem a little odd at first glance—it looks like our first 16 bytes are 0x0100. Virtually everything in an attribute's blob is in little-endian format, so the least significant bits go first. Keep this in mind as we traverse the blob's structure. This might be confusing at first, if you're used to reading binary values from the most significant bits to the least.

> **NOTE** *A compiler has the choice to not store anything about the attribute if a no-argument constructor was used and no named parameters were assigned. The C# compiler will insert the 16-bit prolog, even if it's not necessary; other compilers may decide to put nothing in the parentheses.*

The next value depends on a couple of issues. If a constructor that takes arguments was used, the bytes after the prolog will contain the values of the constructor's arguments. In our case, we have two arguments to decipher. That is why it's required to store which constructor was used in the code, because it's possible to use named properties in an attribute declaration, as was done in Listing A-2. In our case, we need to read the string data first, and then read the integer array. After these arguments are read out of the blob, you would then read the named arguments. This isn't quite as difficult as it sounds, because you know how many arguments the constructor needs. After you've finished reading that constructor data (which we'll get to in the next paragraph), you know you have named properties to deal with if there is still some information in the byte stream.

Let's get back to our attribute's bytes. The next value is 0x0F, or 15. We know that our first argument to the constructor is a string, so this must have something to do with the string. However, this value corresponds to a character that didn't exist in our given string ("My string data."). String data is stored in a format called a SerString. Figure A-1 shows how a SerString is structured.

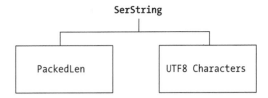

Figure A-1. SerString format

The PackedLen section contains the length of the string, which is used to grab the correct number of bytes, which correspond to UTF8 characters. Note that the PackedLen section is not stored in little-endian format.[3] In the data shown in Listing A-2, reading the string is easy. Figure A-2 illustrates the process.

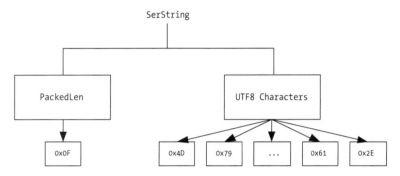

Figure A-2. A 1-byte PackedLen section

0x0F is equal to 15, which is the length of the string data.[4] However, if you store a large string in an attribute, it gets confusing. Take a look at the following class declaration:

```
// 16000 bytes long.
[TestAttribute("1234567890...1234567890." + ... +
    "1234567890...1234567890.", new int[] {2, 3},
    ByteData = 22)]
public class LongStringTestClass {}
```

---

3. In the case where there is only 1 byte to denote the length of the SerString, it's no big deal. This will become important when you start dealing with larger strings.

4. Fortunately, ILDasm will show the attribute byte data as character data in comments, so it's pretty easy to verify that the next 15 bytes are the actual value of the string.

The string is actually 16,000 bytes long (we're not showing the entire string here).[5] The (partial) ILDasm result is this:

```
.custom instance void AttributeFormatting.TestAttribute::.ctor(
  string, int32[]) =
  ( 01 00 BE 80 31 32 33 34 35 36 37 38 39 30 31 32    // ...@123456789012
```

After the prolog, we have 0xBE and 0x80 before we start seeing UTF8 characters that look like what was stored in the string. Obviously, we need to use more than 1 byte of storage to store the string length. But how can we determine what the byte size of PackedLen is going to be? Combining the two byte values isn't the right answer; 0xBE80 equals 48768. There must be a way to evaluate the first byte to determine how many bytes make up the PackedLen value.

The answer lies in the most significant bits of the first PackedLen value. Here are the rules to follow to find the SerString length:

- If the byte value is less than 128 (or 10000000), the length is made up of 1 byte.

- If the byte value is less than 192 (or 11000000), the length is made up of 2 bytes, and the first bit in the first byte is set to zero.

- Otherwise, 4 bytes make up the length, and the first 2 bits in the first byte are set to zero.

Therefore, the longest string that can be represented in a SerString is just over half a billion bytes: 536,870,911.[6] In the case of our second SerString, which is 16,000 characters, the length is determined by subtracting 0x80 from the first byte, which is 0xBE – 0x80, or 0x3E. The second byte is concatenated with this result, which gives us 0x3E80, or 16,000.

 NOTE *The UTF8 characters are also encoded, although if you usually stick to ASCII characters, you won't see this encoding. Characters less than 128 are 1 byte in size, with the last 7 bits containing the value. Characters between 128 and 2047 are 2 bytes in size, with the last 5 bits of the first byte and the last 6 bits of the second byte making up the value. Any value greater than 2048 bytes is stored in 3 bytes, with the last 4 bits in the first byte and the last 6 bits in the second and third bytes making up the value.*

---

5. Note that we needed to use string concatenation to do this. The C# compiler won't accept a string if it's over 2046 characters in length.

6. If you're curious about how this value is calculated, look up the CorSigCompressData() method in cor.h.

The next argument used on TestClass in Listing A-2 is an integer array. An array is encoded with the length of the array first, and then its values, similar to a SerString encoding. However, all of the values of the array (including the length value) are in little-endian format, and the length value is always 4 bytes. Figure A-3 breaks down the structure of our array encoded into the byte stream.

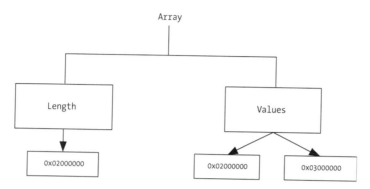

Figure A-3. Array encoding

The array values are stored into their native formats. Note that boolean values are stored as 1-byte values (1 for true and 0 for false).

We've run out of constructor arguments. Now we need to deal with any named parameters that were given. The next 2 bytes after the constructor arguments will tell you how many named parameters were used. In our case, that value is 0x0100, which means one named parameter was given. Note that this value should always be present, so if no named parameters were used, you would see 0x0000. After this 2-byte value, the named parameter information is given. As you would expect, the named parameter needs more information than a simple constructor argument, so attribute readers know which property to set when the attribute is reconstructed. Figure A-4 demonstrates how these named parameters are formatted.

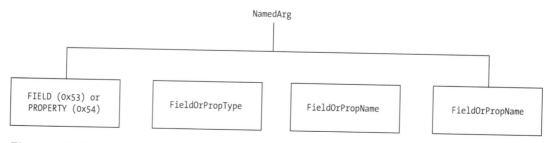

Figure A-4. Named parameter format

The first byte tells you if a field or a property setter should be used. In our case, 0x54 shows up as the first byte, so we know the named parameter is a property. If a public field were used, this value would be 0x53. The second value is an element type value 1 byte in length.[7] Our element type is 0x05, which corresponds to ELEMENT_TYPE_U1, or a byte. The next block of bytes is a SerString that defines the name of the parameter. Not surprisingly, our SerString is equal to "ByteData." Finally, the parameter's value is given. Our value is 1 byte in length: 0x16, which is the value of 22 given in the C# code.

That's it! Let's go through two more examples to review the structure.

```
[TestAttribute(mPublicString = "22")]
public class AnotherTestClass {}
```

Here's the corresponding metadata:

```
.custom instance void
  AttributeFormatting.TestAttribute::.ctor() =
  ( 01 00 01 00 53 0E 0D 6D 50 75 62 6C 69 63 53 74    // ....S..mPublicSt
  72 69 6E 67 02 32 32 )                               // ring.22
```

As always, the prolog makes up the first 2 bytes. Since we used a no-argument constructor, the next 2 bytes will tell us if any named parameters were used. Since that 2-byte value is 0x0100, we know one named argument was used. The next byte is 0x53, which means that a public field's value was set. The element type value is 0x0E, which is the ELEMENT_TYPE_STRING value. That means that the field name's type is a SerString. The next byte is 0x0D, or 13 bytes. Since that value is under 128, the PackedLen value is 1 byte in length. The next 13 bytes make up the UTF8 values of the field name, which is mPublicString. The next byte is the length of the value of the parameter, which is 2 bytes. The last 2 bytes make up the parameter's value, which is 0x32 0x32, or "22."

Here's another example:

```
[TestAttribute()]
public class YetAnotherTestClass {}
```

Not surprisingly, the resulting metadata is pretty sparse.

```
.custom instance void
  AttributeFormatting.TestAttribute::.ctor() = ( 01 00 00 00 )
```

---

7. These values are defined in Section 22.1.15 of Partition II, as well as in corhdr.h.

After the prolog, we check the constructor for argument values. The no-named argument format was used, so now we need to check for named parameters. The next 2 bytes are 0x0000, which means no named parameters need to be set.

SOURCE CODE   *The code for these examples is in AppendixA\AttributeFormatting.*

Although the attribute format may seem a little convoluted at first glance, it's not too bad once you get the hang of it. Fortunately, you'll never spend a lot of time parsing attribute byte arrays. But it's always advantageous to have at least a general understanding of the underpinnings of a technology.

Index

W

Web site address
  for discussions on checked
    exceptions and .NET, 163–164
  for installing the FxCop tool, 177
  for Intertech Training, vii
  for Jason Bock, vii
  for Magenic Technologies, vii
  for source code, xii
Windows API
  Beep() function, 74
  character sets it can handle, 75
Windows Explorer
  assembly information shown in,
    35
Write() method
  implementing a simple tracing
    mechanism with, 30

X

XML serialization
  code for Customer classes updated
    for, 91–92
XML serialization attributes
  table of, 98
  using, 94–98
XML Serializer
  using, 91–94
XmlAnyAttribute attribute
  function of, 98

XmlAnyElement attribute
  function of, 98
XmlArray attribute
  controlling serialization of an array
    of objects with, 96
  function of, 98
XmlArrayItem attribute
  function of, 98
XmlAttribute attribute
  function of, 98
XmlChoiceIdentifier attribute
  function of, 98
XmlElement attribute
  function of, 98
XmlEnum attribute
  function of, 98
XmlIgnore attribute
  function of, 98
  use of in code for XML serialization,
    91–93
XmlInclude attribute
  function of, 98
XmlRoot attribute
  function of, 98
XmlSerializer class
  vs. BinaryFormatter and
    SoapFormatter classes, 91
  code showing use of, 93
XmlText attribute
  function of, 98
XmlType attribute
  function of, 98

forums.apress.com
FOR PROFESSIONALS BY PROFESSIONALS™

JOIN THE APRESS FORUMS AND BE PART OF OUR COMMUNITY. You'll find discussions that cover topics of interest to IT professionals, programmers, and enthusiasts just like you. If you post a query to one of our forums, you can expect that some of the best minds in the business—especially Apress authors, who all write with *The Expert's Voice™*—will chime in to help you. Why not aim to become one of our most valuable participants (MVPs) and win cool stuff? Here's a sampling of what you'll find:

DATABASES
Data drives everything.
Share information, exchange ideas, and discuss any database programming or administration issues.

PROGRAMMING/BUSINESS
Unfortunately, it is.
Talk about the Apress line of books that cover software methodology, best practices, and how programmers interact with the "suits."

INTERNET TECHNOLOGIES AND NETWORKING
Try living without plumbing (and eventually IPv6).
Talk about networking topics including protocols, design, administration, wireless, wired, storage, backup, certifications, trends, and new technologies.

WEB DEVELOPMENT/DESIGN
Ugly doesn't cut it anymore, and CGI is absurd.
Help is in sight for your site. Find design solutions for your projects and get ideas for building an interactive Web site.

JAVA
We've come a long way from the old Oak tree.
Hang out and discuss Java in whatever flavor you choose: J2SE, J2EE, J2ME, Jakarta, and so on.

SECURITY
Lots of bad guys out there—the good guys need help.
Discuss computer and network security issues here. Just don't let anyone else know the answers!

MAC OS X
All about the Zen of OS X.
OS X is both the present and the future for Mac apps. Make suggestions, offer up ideas, or boast about your new hardware.

TECHNOLOGY IN ACTION
Cool things. Fun things.
It's after hours. It's time to play. Whether you're into LEGO® MINDSTORMS™ or turning an old PC into a DVR, this is where technology turns into fun.

OPEN SOURCE
Source code is good; understanding (open) source is better.
Discuss open source technologies and related topics such as PHP, MySQL, Linux, Perl, Apache, Python, and more.

WINDOWS
No defenestration here.
Ask questions about all aspects of Windows programming, get help on Microsoft technologies covered in Apress books, or provide feedback on any Apress Windows book.

HOW TO PARTICIPATE:
Go to the Apress Forums site at **http://forums.apress.com/**.
Click the New User link.